TO Clair

Love From

AmY And Angus

xx xxxx* *x

THE GOSPEL ACCORDING TO CHRIS MOYLES

THE GOSPEL ACCORDING TO CHRIS MOYLES

The Story Of A Man And His Mouth

EBURY
PRESS

5 7 9 10 8 6 4

Published in 2006 by Ebury Press, an imprint of Ebury Publishing

Ebury Publishing is a division of the Random House Group

The Random House Group Limited Reg. No. 954009

Addresses for companies within the Random House Group can be found at www.randomhouse.co.uk

A CIP catalogue record for this book is available from the British Library

The Random House Group Limited makes every effort to ensure that the papers used in our books
are made from trees that have been legally sourced from well-managed and credibly certified forests.
Our paper procurement policy can be found on www.randomhouse.co.uk

Interior designed and typeset by seagulls.net

Printed and bound in Great Britain by Mackays of Chatham Plc

ISBN 0091914175

ISBN (from Jan 2007) 9780091914172

This book is dedicated to:

My Mum and Dad. Thank you for EVERYTHING.

My Brother Kieron who's the best brother I ever had.

Sophie for having to read aloud everything I wrote for this book.

Every broadcaster who inspired me, and,

'Anybody that knows me!'

CONTENTS

FORE

WORD

Some might say Chris Moyles and I have a lot in common. We both have big mouths.

I first met Chris when I was a guest on his Radio 1 breakfast show a few years ago. Then in June 2006 we met again, this time as contestant and judge on *X Factor, Battle of the Stars*.

I was actually amazed Chris had agreed to take part. I feared the worst, but when I first heard him sing and watched him perform I was impressed and incredibly grateful that he'd agree to go on the show.

Chris is a brilliant DJ. I wouldn't say his singing is as good but he is a born entertainer. He showed another side to me and the public on the *X Factor* – he's also a very nice guy. His mum came along every night and you could tell how important that relationship is to him. I wish he'd won, but some of his song choices were simply terrible.

Unlike other DJs who have shot to fame and then imploded through ego (although his is quite large) and abuse of their power, Chris is here to stay. I like Chris Moyles, and if you like him you will love this book. I'd buy it.

Simon Cowell, 2006

1

FIRST THINGS FIRST

Hello. My name is Chris Moyles and I am the author of this book! I've never written a book before, but chances are that neither have you, so we're kind of in the same position. In fact, I have never even tried to write a book before.

I'll tell you why and how and all that stuff, after I have explained something first. I love to give background information when telling stories. I like to explain who people are and what they're like before telling a story. I just think it makes for a better reaction when people can imagine them in their heads and get an image of them. This will, I hope, excuse often long-winded stories that get off the subject. With that in mind, I will now try to explain quickly how the hell I got to write a book.

I am a radio DJ on BBC Radio 1, every morning from 7 to 10 a.m.

Most national radio DJs have an agent.

I have an agent.

An agent's job is to find you the right work
at the right price and manage your career.

They actually take a percentage of your wage
and wait for the phone to ring.

The phone rang; it was some publishing company.

I meet with the publishing company (a nice girl called Claire).

She asks me if I have ever thought about writing a book.

I say yes and tell her the idea.

She tells me to go away and try to write twenty pages.

So here I am. I've almost finished the first eight pages. This shit is easy.

Now my idea was to write a fake autobiography. I thought it would be funny. Then I thought that I would make half of it the truth, and the other half all lies. However, after leaving the meeting with the publishing people, I decided just to write a book explaining how to get a publishing deal with a top publishing house. Now that's done, I only have nineteen pages left to write. Told you this shit was easy!

They gave me some books to look at for ideas (I didn't, I sold them). I asked them about the rules of books, page numbers, photographs, etc. For example, any photographs used in this book have to be in black and white because this is cheaper. What an incentive to get me to write a book. I hadn't written a word and they're already telling me they've got no money and any money they do have is not going to be wasted on colour pictures in my book! Anyway, we had a good chat, and then I left their office and went home. It got me thinking about books and the fun you can have. So let's play a while first before I tell you more stuff.

THE

END

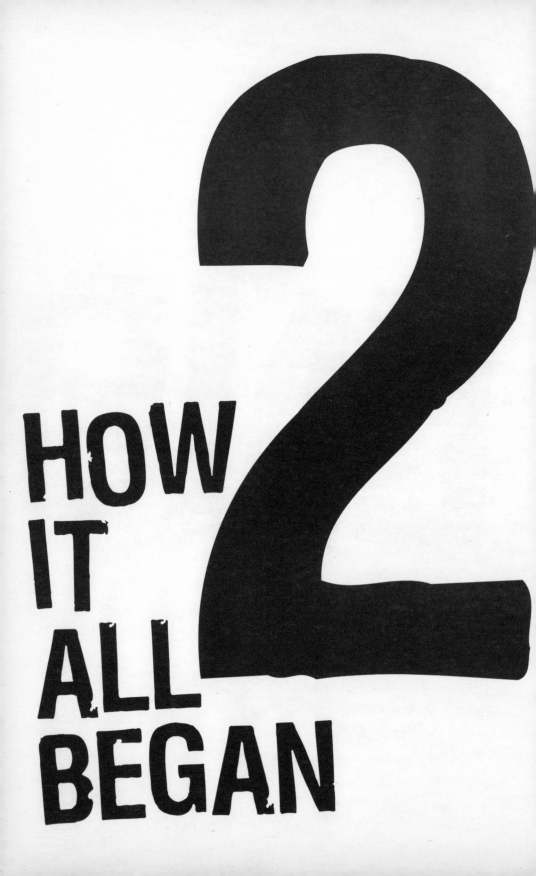

2

HOW IT ALL BEGAN

This isn't going to be a normal autobiography. I've read a few and they often contain lots of boring pages. Things about where they grew up and what their family life was like and those types of things. But I know there are some people who like to read that stuff, so here goes.

I was born in Leeds in West Yorkshire on 22 February 1974. My mum and dad were and still are brilliant parents. I have an older brother called Kieron. He's cool. I was raised as a Roman Catholic and went to three schools: a primary school run by nuns, a middle school called St Kevin's (my radio partner Dave has always found that very amusing and refers to St Kevin as 'the patron saint of car jacking'), and high school, being the place I did my GCSEs. There you go. All sorted.

I think that is just enough information. You bought this book because you listen to the show or maybe a friend told you it was funny. Now you know where and when I was born. You know I have great parents and one brother I get on really well with. You know my religion and that it affected what school I went to. If you need to know any more than that you are either a con artist or there is something seriously wrong with you. I mean it. If you have any unanswered questions about the first sixteen years of my life, then stop it. You're weird. Become an MP or something.

Another reason I don't want to write lots of old stuff about me is because I have a terrible memory. Seriously – I can't remember anything. I have even asked a friend of mine, Dr Mark Hamilton, if there is such a thing as 'partial amnesia'. He told me no and that I just have a 'shit memory'. Cheers.

I do remember the moment that I discovered radio, though. It was Christmas. I was about eleven years old. Mum was in the kitchen baking mince pies (this kind of background information keeping you happy, weirdos?) and the radio was on. The local station was doing a 'Guess the Christmas Song' competition. That was it. No clues. Just guess the name of the song. I didn't know at the time, but now that I've worked in radio for a while I know that competition meant the DJ couldn't be bothered to do any work for his show that day. Anyway I called the number and I got through.

'Hello, what's your answer?' said the phone answerer.

'Erm, "Frosty the Snowman"!' I squeaked.

'What's your name?'

'It's Chris from Leeds.'

'OK, Chris, hold the line and you'll be on in a minute.'

WOW.

How cool is that? I make one phone call and I'm going be on the radio. I thought this was brilliant. Millions of people were going to hear *me* on the radio. I might even win a prize! Some money or maybe even a car. *Wow*. A car! This is brilliant. I can say hello to all my friends, who will be so jealous that I have just won a car on a radio station for simply picking up the—

'Let's go to line three and Chris. Hello, Chris.'

'Hi.'

'OK, Chris, what do you think the song is?'

'Is it "Frosty the Snowman"?'

'Ahhw. No, it's not, I'm afraid, but try again. Right, let's go to line four. Hello …'

CLICK.

WAS THAT IT?

Where's my money? Where was my mention to all my friends?

WHERE THE FUCK IS MY CAR?

He did say try again though, so I did.

I dial the number again and get straight through. It's local radio, remember, and they're running the most stupid Christmas competition ever. The lines are hardly going to be jammed. Anyway, I get back on air again.

'Is it "Rudolph the Red-nosed Reindeer"?'

'Sorry, Chris, that's not the answer either, but it does have the word *the* in it.'

WHAT?

Are you kidding me? This is the most ridiculous competition ever. With the world's laziest DJ. It could be anything. He might even be making it up. How do I know that I didn't actually get it right, but he just keeps changing the answer? I'm calling up again.

Hang on a second. I can't think of another Christmas song that has the word 'the' in the title. 'Merry Christmas Everyone'? No. 'Jingle Bells'? No. 'I Wish It Could Be Christmas Every Day'? No. 'Rudolph the Red'— No, I've already said that. Shit! I need to think.

'Teatime!' shouts Mum.

'Ahw, come on, Mum. I want to phone up and get on the radio again.'

'No, you've tried twice and now your tea is going to get cold.'

'*Twice*?' shouts Dad. 'How many more times do I have to tell you? That phone is for emergencies only.'

So one tea and several mince pies later I was hooked. I had discovered radio. It had been there all this time and I had never realised how much fun it could be. This is the life for me.

After that, I used to listen to and call any radio station I could to try and get on air. I wasn't bothered about winning anything. I just wanted to get on air. Talking on the radio. How cool was that?

So you see I remember that incident very clearly. I remember the mince pies. I remember not finding out what the answer was. Everything. Yet still I've forgotten the name of the woman at the publishing house who asked me to write a book. Partial amnesia. It's got to exist.

Incidentally, I never did find out the answer. Lazy bastard disc jockey.

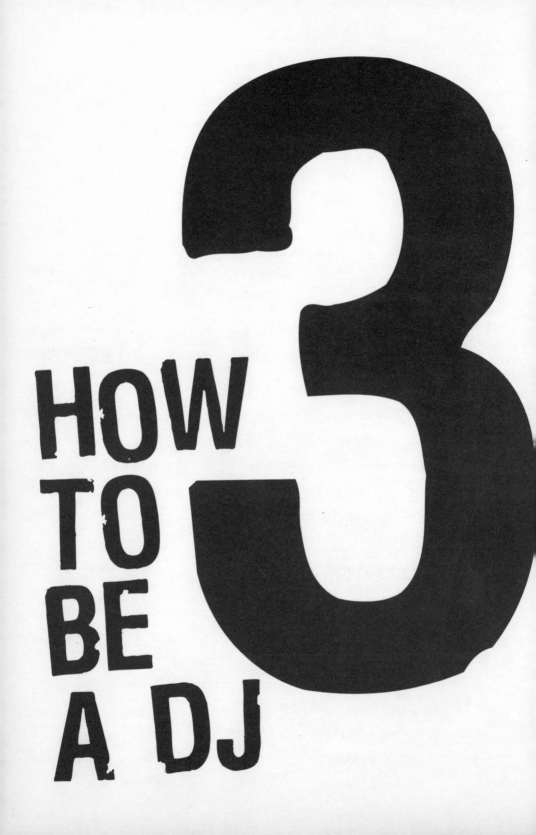

3

HOW TO BE A DJ

B efore I go on, let me tell you this.

I FUCKING LOVE GREAT RADIO!

I really do. Don't get me wrong, I don't love *all* radio. But it's fair to say that when it's done properly I love it. It's the same when you hear a song by a band you love and you love that too. When there's a TV series you've been watching that you just can't miss. The same feeling you get when you have no plans for the night and two of your best mates call you and tell you they're in your local pub. I love that feeling. Unless they call you when your favourite TV show is about to start … but I think you've got my point. Now let me tell you something else.

I MAKE FUCKING GREAT RADIO.

I do. Maybe not every link, because you have to remember I'm on air fifteen hours a week. That's sixty hours of new stuff every month. However, I must say that, for the most part, I am great at making great radio. Many people try and fail. Lots of people have their moments. Only a few people on the radio make great radio. I am high on that list. Sounds arrogant? Absolutely. But why not? I have done this shit since I was twelve years old. I have done hospital radio from a mental hospital. I have worked at a radio station that wasn't even on the radio but broadcasting to a shop. I have even worked in Stoke-on-Trent! Trust me. I've learnt how to do this stuff.

The question people ask me is what advice can I give them.

WHY THE HELL WOULD I TELL THEM?

Seriously, why would I give away all my thoughts and all the learning that I've spent fifteen years finding out? For free?! I don't think so. However, I have a book to write and a lot of empty pages to fill, so I will go against my better judgement and tell you why I think I make great radio, and how to do it.

Here's the secret, and trust me, it's a let-down, but it's the truth.

First, you need to be born to be good at radio. Crappy, I know, but it's the truth. If you're reading this and you think you have what it takes to be a brilliant broadcaster, let me be the first to tell you. You probably don't. I mean, you can't just be good at something, unless you are, and if that's the case, you're halfway there. Look at all the people who think they can sing and audition for *X Factor*. They're rubbish. Just 'cos you have a go doesn't mean you'll be good at it.

The second thing is a little bit easier, and I'm slightly reluctant to tell you.

I have learnt how to do great radio from listening to great radio. James Whale was one of the first broadcasters I noticed was great. One of the reasons for this is he tells you he's great. How genius is that? But think about it. He knows more about radio than the listener does, so who's to argue with him? Kenny Everett was also a genius. He would spend hours working on something that may last thirty seconds. But it was worth it if it made you smile or laugh out loud. You have to put the effort in; this shit doesn't always come easy. Simon Mayo I have always admired. He makes listening to him effortless. Howard Stern is somebody who will say stuff that makes me belly-laugh. He also says the stuff that nobody else says. Nick Abbot used to do a late-night phone-in show on Virgin Radio. A great myth about me is that I used to call up, putting on strange accents and trying to be funny, when I was out of work. It's true. I did. Nick was brilliant with callers. He wouldn't talk to them as if they were his friends. They weren't. They were strangers calling into a radio station. I can't explain it, but he had something special in the way he spoke to them. Steve Wright, who helped me a lot – more on that later – is also brilliant. So different from all of the above. He creates a little special world just for you and him, while talking to everybody and ignoring the 'talk to one listener' theory.

So, you take all these great radio people.

THEN YOU STEAL FROM THEM.

Really, that's what you do. It takes time, though, because for a while you just try to copy them, badly. Eventually you start to do your own thing, but the influences are buried deep and there's nothing you can do about it.

I must admit I thought for a while before admitting the above, until it occurred to me that:

MOST OF THE ABOVE PEOPLE STOLE AS WELL.

James Whale has influences from Stern.

Steve Wright has influences from Rick Dees in the US.

Nick Abbot had influences from Neil Rogers in the US.

So the way I look at it, it's all fair game.

People ask me what station I listen to and I tell them Radio 1. I really do. I wouldn't want to work there if the station was rubbish.

Scott Mills is brilliant. We share a lot of the same humour but he does his show very differently to me. It's great because I can listen as a listener and totally forget I know him. He's funny off the air as well. We didn't hit it off at first and it was actually Sophie, my girlfriend, who kind of got us together. She was working with him on the TV and kept telling me what a top bloke he was. Eventually I gave in and agreed. He is brilliant live as well. If he ever plays near you, go and see him. But don't buy him a drink after the gig – by then he'll have had enough already!

I also really admire Vernon Kay. I used to hate him on the TV. Dave and I would refer to him as 'Vermin Kay', but I've got to say, on the radio he's ace. His stories are great and I love the way he gets really excited about stuff. He's also a top bloke and a great friend. I've got a lot of time for Vernon. He called me at home to tell me about his TV deal in the States. He had just come back from signing a deal with NBC in Los Angeles and I was bouncing off the walls with excitement for him. I swear I was more excited than he was. He'd just got back home and was on his own in the living room having a beer and watching some random football match with Sunderland. Meanwhile, his wife was chatting to a friend in the kitchen. That's another reason why I like Vernon. He has a hot wife. Top marks, fella. Although he doesn't come out to drink with us that much because Tess tells him off. (He'll kill me for putting that in.) Love you, pal. And your Mrs too.

4
THE
RADIO 1
TEAM

started working for Radio 1 back in 1997, and I've worked with some brilliant people. Don't get me wrong, I've also worked with some shite, but there are some top names on the list.

Jeff Smith is the man responsible for my joining Radio 1. If it wasn't for Jeff Smith, I genuinely believe I would never have got to work for Radio 1. Thanks, mate.

When the BBC put me on the early shift, they also gave me two people to work with. The rule at the time was that most programmes were given a producer and a broadcast assistant (BA). My first-ever producer was a guy called Simon Barnett. Simon was sold to me as being one of the freshest, most creative talents in the building. I was naturally excited.

'What shows has he worked on so far?' I asked.

'Well, he's just finished working with Lisa I'Anson at lunchtimes.'

The excitement didn't last long.

Now I must point out that I grew to like Lisa a lot. As far as radio skills went, not the best in the world maybe. A great voice but didn't really know how to use it. The show was like listening to a bunch of overly hip London trendsetters. It said nothing to me about my life in Leeds or even Milton Keynes. With such features as 'Where's Da Party At', the show seemed to be aimed at a London female who loves her R 'n' B and going shopping with her platinum card down Bond Street. So naturally when I turned up at Radio 1:

THEY GAVE ME THE GUY WHO DID THAT SHOW!

As it turned out Simon was a nice guy. He was a decent fella who let me do some sketches and be myself. We were assisted in this task by Jude Adam. Jude, bless her, talks. She talks, a lot. So much so that she wasn't the kind of girl you'd choose to work with at three o'clock in the morning. However, it worked well enough and Jude turned out to be a little star.

Simon quickly moved on and in his place came a man called Ben Cooper. Ben turned out to be one of *the* most important people in my success at Radio 1. And he still is. Ben is a few years older than me, but we seemed to share the same sense of humour. We got on immediately. He was straight, yet funny. Older, yet as childish. We had such a laugh in the early mornings, and then in the afternoons. Ben is now one of my bosses and was instrumental in getting me on the breakfast show. He is bloody brilliant at radio. (Kiss kiss, slurp slurp.) We also worked on the Radio 1 road shows together. Was that fun? You have no idea. Trust me. Travelling the week in a Winnebago to towns you'd never heard off with an old guy driving at 75 m.p.h. through country lanes he really can't see? Priceless. For two summers, Ben, Comedy Dave and I were on the road for six days playing to an average of 75,000 people. Meeting rock stars in such places as Great Yarmouth and Hunstanton. Brilliant.

COMEDY DAVE

I suppose I better write a little bit about the legend that is Comedy Dave. Many people think that Dave and I had worked together for years before joining Radio 1. The truth is that we met *at* Radio 1. He used to do technical bits at the station, and in the days of Mark and Lard at breakfast, the show came from Manchester. Dave had the task of fading the news up every half hour. What a job.

As he was in the building every morning at 6 o'clock, we quickly became pals and one day Dave told me that he had some ideas he thought were funny. We'd often go to the pub together, so one day I took a look at the ideas and they made me laugh out loud. They were odd to say the least. One of them was a daily tribute to the band Candyflip. Candyflip were not very famous, and were mostly known for a cover version of 'Strawberry Fields Forever' by the Beatles, which charted for them back in 1990. A daily tribute to a band that had had *one* hit, with a cover version of a song that some saw as sacrilege: this was my kind of guy!

Dave started coming into work early and hanging out in the studio with me and Ben. As time went on, he started coming in earlier, and making more appearances on the show. Eventually he became BA on the programme and the rest, as they say, is history.

Now, get ready for a treat. This is the real story on how Dave became known as Comedy Dave.

When I met him, a guy in the building had already nicknamed him 'Super Dave'. I didn't like it. Then one day, comedian Lee Hurst was on the show. Dave was chipping in as usual and Lee asked who he was.

'That's Super Dave,' I told him.

'Comedy Dave more like,' said Lee sarcastically.

THAT'S IT. NOW YOU KNOW.

Dave and I are still great mates, despite the fact that he has started branching out. He has begun presenting shows with another sidekick character called Mark 'Chappers' Chapman. It's like having kids, I suppose. You have to let them go off and do their thing before they realise how good they've had it all along and come crawling back. (He'll hate that!)

Dave writes a lot of the stuff we do on the show – in fact, pretty much all the written stuff. Incidentally, when we started doing the breakfast show, he gave himself the title Director of Comedy.

Comedy Dave indeed!

I love working with Dave, I really do. Now sometimes he can be a right royal pain in the arse. He can, at times, be a stubborn little git who doesn't really wanna play or talk about a certain subject. This often makes for some quite spicy radio. Other times, it can lead us down a dead end. And trust me I go down enough of them on my own! But 95 per cent of the time it all works perfectly. The main reason I like working with Dave is that we have a laugh. It's something you don't really appreciate that much when you do it on a daily basis. However, when you think about it, our daily routine, our job, involves me and a group of my mates laughing, a lot. I get to have a laugh with my mate Dave five days a week. What a brilliant job! Unless he's in a grumpy mood. Or I'm in a grumpy mood. Or the rest of the team are in a grumpy mood, but more on that later.

There is a lot of eye contact between us. That makes us sound a bit girlie but it really helps with the timing of the show. It means we don't talk over each other so much and it allows us to indicate to each other when one wants to jump in on a link. After a certain amount of time working together, this kind of thing happens naturally and most of the time we don't even notice. Probably just as well – I wouldn't like to think that I stare into the eyes of my red-blooded male friend for three hours a day just to make a living.

There have been a lot of stories told about Dave on air since 1997. One of my favourite ones, which has been used quite a bit on the show, was when he made the biggest balls-up in his career, and completely got away with it.

Did he swear on air?

No. Although he did swear on air once. Or maybe twice. But that's not the story.

Has he been told off by management for being drunk with a competition winner?

Well, yes, actually, but that's not it either.

Has he given out a line-up on air for a concert, when it wasn't meant to be announced for another few days?

Yes, he has. This he has done a few times, to be fair. It's hard to trust him with certain bits of information sometimes.

Has he announced somebody on air as being dead, when they're still alive? And currently on tour?

Yes.

Has he had a certain charity for the deaf screaming for my head on a plate because he made comments about a guy doing sign language at a Spice Girls concert?

Yes.

Has he written a spoof advert for a brand of fish products by Aunt Fanny that began with the words 'Everybody loves fish, but no one quite makes fish like Fanny's'?

Yes, and once again, I got the blame.

Has he said on air that all ugly women should be sterilised so that no more ugly babies can be born?

Yes. Hitler would've been proud!

No, it's none of those stories, although they are all corkers and may be written up one day in a follow-up book entitled: *My mate Dave, he can be a bit of a dopey twat.* My favourite story about Dave is as follows and is completely true.

One day I was sitting at my desk at Radio 1. I hadn't been there that long and don't think Dave and I were working together properly yet. The radio on my desk is on and I'm listening to Simon Mayo, who was on air that morning doing his show as normal. Suddenly my radio goes quiet. I reach for the volume knob and turn it up. Often DJs switch the wrong CD off and after a second or two it will start again from the beginning. Mayo rarely made mistakes like this but it happens to us all. After five or six seconds, I looked up to see a few other faces in the office also looking as confused as I was. Three seconds later, I knew there was a problem. I jumped up from my desk and ran out of the office towards the stairs to the studio. Now, just exactly what I was going to do, I had no idea. What can I tell you

– it was just a Superman instinct. Anyway, I bump into one of the bosses and it now seems there is a serious problem. As I get to the studio area, Dave is coming out of a room. A room he really shouldn't have been in. A room I've never seen him in since.

'What's going on?' asks Dave.

'We're off the air!' I proclaimed.

'What?'

'Mayo's just gone off air. Dead silence. Don't know what happened.'

At this point Dave's face drops a little. And he turns a little bit white. You know, Michael Jackson colour.

'What were you doing in there, Dave?'

Without any hesitation Dave replies, 'I was just moving some wires around.'

'Dave, have you taken us off air?'

He insists that he hasn't and also states what a weird coincidence it was that he was pulling wires out of the wall at the same time that we went off air.

I hover outside the studio. Mayo looks puzzled. The producer is on the phone to the control room at Broadcasting House. The boss is running round not really knowing what to do. After a few more minutes, Dave quietly walks back into the room he shouldn't have been in, and, strangely, music begins coming out of the speakers again all round the building. Dave pops his head out of the door and gives me one of those looks that simply tells me:

COMEDY DAVE TOOK RADIO 1 OFF THE AIR – FOR FIFTEEN MINUTES.

Now, there are many ways in which you can balls up at a radio station, but surely taking the entire radio station *off the air for fifteen minutes* has got to be a balls-up on a massive scale. And that's another reason why I love him. Top man.

RACHEL JONES

A lot of regular listeners to the show don't realise that Aled and Rachel share a surname. However, Rachel will be the first one to tell you that they are in no way whatsoever related. The relationship these two have really gets on my nerves. Rachel is like Aled's older sister. One minute she loves him to bits, constantly telling me how hard he's working and how brilliant he is. The next, she's making him feel two inches tall, telling him off in her booming Kidderminster voice, saying things like:

'Aled, why didn't you check it? I told you to check it, Aled.'

I tell you, it's like living in an awful ITV sitcom some days.

Rachel has been producer of the morning show since we began in January 2004. She was first choice on a list that contained her name only. We started working together when we did Saturday mornings. Many people at the time said it was our finest hour. This used to piss me off, as Dave and I both did *zero* work for the show, with me often turning up at 9.59 a.m. for a ten o'clock start, a condition I called 'Sixth-shift Syndrome'. Rachel didn't actually produce the show then. She was the BA to a guy called Richard Murdoch. He was another nice guy and a great producer.

He went on to produce Sara Cox at breakfast and then Colin (Murray) and Edith (Bowman) at lunchtime. What a bunch of egos that is to work with! Me, Coxy and Colin and Edith. Not on your worst enemy. And he's still a really nice bloke. (Richard would often turn up for a Saturday-morning shift with red-stained teeth from drinking red wine the night before. Because of this Dave nicknamed him 'Count Drunkula'. Genius.) The weird thing was that if you had turned up on any given Saturday, you'd have thought Rachel produced the show. She was very – how can I put it? – vocal. We had meetings every week that she would pretty much lead. She had ideas on what features we should do and what guests to book. We had an amazing list of guests from Jerry Springer to S Club 7 (oh yes, I ain't kidding!). The show was a lot of fun, but hard work to do, with Dave and me often hanging from the night before.

Some of my favourite features on the show included 'Girls Going to Football'. And then there was the obvious follow-up: 'Boys Going Shopping'. We had bit for blokes who were in shit with their other halves called 'Who's In The Doghouse', where Dave and I would give the callers a valid excuse to tell their Mrs why they had come from the pub at four in the morning stinking of booze. Add in our Saturday-morning wedding feature 'May Divorce Be With You' and the show was a big hit.

Rachel was absolutely part of the success.

After a while we jacked in the Saturday show and Rachel went off to do other stuff. Eventually, in 2003, we were looking for another producer to work with us on the award-winning afternoon show. Rachel was our first choice and we got to work. As we'd done the show for five years, we knew where we were going. On her first show as new producer, Rachel jokingly moaned and whined all the way through the show. Our audience were not impressed.

'Who the fuck is this moaning little cow?'

'Tell that Brummie to stop her whining.'

'Hey, Moyles, if you wanna get lap-dancers in the studio, do it. Fuck that silly bitch.'

I love our audience. They're so ... open!

I took Rachel out for a drink and explained that she'd have to relax a little. Our audience were very used to our style and didn't much like strangers coming and spoiling it. Rachel understood and the next day was a different person. The audience turned and began liking her. The irony is that now Rachel moans more than ever, and the audience bloody love her. They even moan at me if I have a go at her. Fickle bastards.

Rachel is really lovely. I know I keep saying this about the team but I mean it. Why would I work with somebody that I didn't like? Rachel was our *only* choice to produce the breakfast show. I knew that she would be the right person for the job. The team were all hand-picked. Al. Rachel. Dominic. I knew what I wanted to do at breakfast and that it was going to be tough, and I knew exactly who would help me make it a big hit. My boss Andy Parfitt will hate me telling this story, but before we started the show, he took me out and explained to me that the figures would fall when we got our first ratings in. He knew he was making the right decision but warned us that this was merely a trend in radio-listening figures when a new show started and that it would take a while to build. I asked him what he would do if the figures didn't fall.

'Oh that would be great. We'd all have a good drink.'

'What if the figures went up a bit?'

'We'd have a bigger drink and be very drunk indeed.'

'Andy, what if the figures go up, by a lot?' I asked.

'THEN WE'D END UP IN THE GUTTER FOR A WEEK.'

Our first set of official figures came in and we had increased the audience by 640,000 listeners. We're still owed the gutter week.

Rachel was very much responsible for that increase. Mainly I was, you understand, but Rachel was a big help too. She has a good ear for radio and is very creative. Sometimes she doesn't get the show as much as Aled or Dave. She'll worry about saying certain things on air but she knows what sounds funny and pretty much trusts me. And damn right she should. I've trusted her on three shows of mine so far, this being the biggest one.

I smile every time we go out on the road and she gets recognised. She still finds it a bit odd and sometimes embarrassing. 'Which one is Rachel?' will be the cry. It's nice that the audience like her so much. I just wish they'd stop moaning at me for picking on her. Trust me: she needs to be kept in her place sometimes. I've got one of the smallest egos on the team. Rachel can be a right diva. What's funny is that she has no idea that she can be a diva. Seriously, *no idea whatsoever.*

Once again, and I swear this is true, the last words I heard from her when I left work today were the following:

'I'm just putting my expenses in and I tell you what. They better bloody pay me or there'll be trouble.'

Trust me, they'll pay her.

ALED HAYDN JONES

Aled is a really, really nice guy. With the exception of Dave, he's been working with me the longest. He's a hard worker who has got better and better with the ideas and creativity he brings to the show. He also understands the show a hell of a lot. He knows that it's a good laugh and he's always OK with us ripping him on air and taking the piss out of him. That said, though, he went through a long phase of having a major concern with the show. This has *never* been mentioned on the air, but I'm going to tell you this because I think it's funny. I also want to tell you because he pissed me off for years with this particular problem and I want you to know the hell I go through on a daily basis with members of my team. You see, everybody knows that I'm the bad guy on air. Moyles is the bully. Moyles is the ego. Moyles is the one who always wants his own way. Moyles is the lazy one. Moyles is the one who gets away with murder.

IT'S TIME TO PUT THINGS STRAIGHT.

It's not the easiest job in the world doing what we all do. But let's be honest about it. We ain't picking up other people's rubbish and throwing it into the back of a big smelly old truck. We're not on our feet all day working in a supermarket telling brainless morons where the milk or frozen pizzas are. We make radio. Great radio. We spend several hours a day making great radio that over eight million people tune in to every week. It's not the hardest job in the world. However, sometimes you would think that these people are organising peace talks with NATO. I really mean it. They constantly moan at how much work they have to do. They moan about deadlines and turning things round for the show on time.

They demand days off in lieu. When they're in a bad mood, they don't hide it and get on with things, they let you know, in no uncertain terms, that they are in a bad mood. That they didn't get enough sleep the night before or that they have to travel three hours to get to some place where we're doing a Radio 1 event. They moan about the fact that they have to call BBC Transport to book some cars to pick them up from the train station and drive them to the hotel that Radio 1 are paying for. They moan about the fact that they haven't received the new Madonna CD yet. Which they'll get for free, before it's even been released to the public.

YET I'M THE GRUMPY EGO THAT ALWAYS WANTS HIS OWN WAY!

It's unbelievable. I swear, as I write this today, we have just had a meeting about a forthcoming outside broadcast. It's going to be for Christmas day and will be recorded at singer Charlotte Church's mother's pub in Cardiff. We'll do a silly Christmas quiz and some karaoke. That is agreed. That's the show we are doing. However, this morning, Rachel, our fine producer, has just told us categorically that she will not do any karaoke whatsoever. I have to do it. Dave has to do it. Aled has to do it. Rachel though, no, she doesn't want to … *BECAUSE SHE MIGHT GET EMBARRASSED!*

This is a woman who has had her private life discussed on air. Who has had her breast size discussed on air. This is a woman who any time she seems to be in a bad mood will be asked if her 'special friends' are visiting. In front of eight million people. Every day. But God forbid that she sings 'Up Where We Belong' in a pub of twenty-five strangers.

You see, it's not always as easy as it seems. Working so closely with these brilliant people ain't always a walk in the park. I mean, these people have got so many issues and throw so many wobblers that they make me look like fucking Snow White. Here are some more quick examples on why my team are such hard work sometimes, before I tell you the Aled issue.

* Rhys Hughes, our executive producer, once got so frustrated with me that he kicked a door and knocked a picture off the wall.

* Rachel is so insecure. No matter how many times I tell her that she is *the best* producer in radio and that I don't want to do the show without her, she still regularly tells me that I don't appreciate her.

* Natasha, who used to work on the show, once screwed up so badly that when we were due to play a world exclusive of the new Sugarbabes single she gave us the wrong track, and I was informed I wasn't allowed to tell her off about it, because, and I quote, 'She's lovely'!

* Dave, who works in a state-of-the-art studio and has his own hydraulic desk that can be set to any height, refuses to stand up, because he gets 'Too tired'.

Honestly, if you think I seem like hard work, try hanging out with these people on a daily basis. That said, though, and I really mean this:

I BLOODY LOVE THEM ALL AND WOULD HATE TO LOSE ANY OF THEM. THEY ARE THE BEST RADIO TEAM IN THE HISTORY OF THE BBC. (AND THEY ALL DESERVE A PAY RISE AND A DAY OFF IN LIEU.)

Anyway, back to Aled.

Aled is Welsh. He is a good-looking lad who is a hard worker and is really fun to be around, most of the time. I say most of the time, because every so often Aled has some kind of brain seizure, where he loses all sense of reality. If you ever heard Aled on air, you might have assumed he was gay.

You might have come to this conclusion after listening to him say that Britney and Madonna are his favourite acts. That he uses Dove Body Silk on a daily basis or that he won't be photographed unless he's had a shave and a haircut. He dances in the studio to any camp pop track; he hates rock music, but loves *The OC*, and he drinks a cocktail called a Woo Woo. So imagine my surprise when Aled says that he needs a word with me. We go into a quiet little office, where he tells me that he's worried that some of our listeners might think he's a poof.

ARE YOU FUCKING KIDDING ME?

Aled has to be one of the gayest people I have ever met. He looks gay. He sounds gay. He talks gay. HE IS GAY.

'I'm just worried that some of the audience might think that I'm gay,' said Aled.

I looked right into his camp little eyes and told him, 'Aled, there is not one person on the face of this earth who doesn't know that you are gay.'

It doesn't happen often, but it did that day. It turned out I was wrong. There was someone on the planet who didn't know he was gay. In fact, two people: his grandparents.

'I just don't think I'm ready to come out on air yet,' he proclaimed.

'Aled, this morning you were singing Shirley Bassey songs and saying how "well" Will Young looks on his new video.'

What you need to understand about Aled is that he gets a little bit hyper sometimes. For a guy who visits Starbucks about five times a day it's no wonder. He worries about things and lets himself get all worked up over them, and this was one of those things. To be fair, I realise what a huge thing it is to 'come out' to your friends and family, especially maybe the older generation. I have never had a problem with anybody's sexuality. Some of my best friends know some gay people. However, after a while I understood what his concerns were and we talked about it. And talked about it. And talked some more about it.

'Aled, what are you so worried about?'

'Well, I don't want people thinking that I'm the Welsh poof on the show.'

'But you are,' I said. (Really, I am so tactful; I should've been a counsellor or something.)

The fact is that our listeners are very blunt and to the point. I am the funny fat bastard. Rachel is either the sexy one, or the one with the whining Kidderminster accent. Aled is the Welsh gay one. It's just the way our loving radio audience refer to us. It doesn't mean they don't like us. In fact, I would say that, for a lot of the listeners, Aled is their favourite member of the team.

Luckily the Aled situation was resolved. One day, on a train back from Wales, he informs me that he's decided what he's going to do. He's made his mind up and even has a master plan. He won't say on the air that he is gay. However, if the team are having a discussion about girlfriends or boyfriends, then he wants to join in and maybe slip into the conversation that his boyfriend also loves watching 24 or whatever the subject is, great. I'm happy if he's happy. It's taken us twelve months to get to this point, but whatever makes the little fella's life easier. So it's agreed, no song and dance about it (which was my suggestion, an actual song sung by Al saying that he's coming out). He would simply casually mention something one day on air.

The very next day, mid-link about what we all did the night before, Aled suddenly blurts out:

'I have a boyfriend and we just watched TV!'

Brilliant. That would've sounded so natural! I didn't know what to make of it. I knew he didn't want me to react to it, so Dave, Rachel and I just looked at each other and carried on with the link. The best bit was all the text messages that came in, with pretty much every one saying:

'Did Aled just say he has a boyfriend? Who would've thought it?!'

DOMINIC BYRNE – THE VOICE OF NEWS

Dom is brilliant. I love him. I don't love him in a gay way – how could I? He's bald – but I love him in many other ways. He is the best newsreader on the radio anywhere in the world. That is the truth. I can't think of anybody who could do a better job for the show than Dominic Byrne. (Perhaps I do love him in a gay way!)

Dom started at Radio 1 in 1997, the same year that I joined. By October 1998 I was doing the afternoon show with Dave and we had a female reader called Georgina Bowman. If George was ill or on holiday, Dom would often fill in for her. I liked his style straight away. He has a great news-reading voice that isn't too patronising or too light. He is such a professional that he rarely makes mistakes or screws his words up. I was probably most impressed with the way in which he would talk to me on air with so much ease. He could switch from being serious, reading the

1

news, to joking and messing about with us. He did this so seamlessly that I still don't know how he does it. One second he's discussing girls we liked on *Baywatch*, the next he's talking about the government's policies on nuclear air pollution or whatever it may be. Now that may seem an easy task, but trust me, reading the news on my show and then talking to me afterwards caused me so many problems in the past it's unreal. I will explain.

For some reason, I had, and in some respects still do have, a reputation for being difficult and argumentative. However, I think that this statement is absolute bollocks and I will fight anybody who says otherwise. But that was the perception of me at that time. I was told by a senior boss of Radio 1 *Newsbeat*, our catchy, hip and trendy name for the newsroom, that he found it difficult to find people who could read the news on our show. I asked him to explain and he told me there were five points that he had to take into account when finding a replacement for George. Each candidate needed to:

HAVE A GOOD VOICE

BE ABLE TO WRITE THE NEWS

BE ABLE TO THINK ON THEIR FEET

BE ABLE TO 'HANDLE' ME

NOT BE INTIMIDATED BY ME

I just thought it was down to who he decided to put on that particular shift that week. How wrong I was. I explained that Dominic was a perfect fill-in for George. However, this particular boss told me that, as much as he liked Dom, he only had two of those qualities. Two? How rude. Thank God he liked him. At least he scored two out of five. I thought these were professional journalists who could handle any situation when it came to the compiling and delivery of up-to-the-minute news and information. I didn't think it was about how they could handle a quick quip from a smart-arse presenter like myself. Once again I found myself explaining that I *wasn't* the smart-arsed DJ who liked to make newsreaders look stupid. Of course he understood that but still felt that the 'right person' had to be found.

Meanwhile, I *knew* we had the right person. When Radio 1 offered me the breakfast show, I immediately knew who I wanted to read my news. Mr Five-out-of-five himself, Dominic Byrne. Coincidently, Dom once had the same conversation with one of his bosses that I had with one of mine. He was also told that he would never, ever, read the news on the breakfast show on Radio 1.

SCORE: MOYLES 1 – MANAGEMENT 0

Dominic makes me laugh. Out loud. This has always been a bit of a test for me. It's strange, even if I find something very funny, I might not laugh out loud once. If something does make me laugh out loud, I pretty much always remember it. *The Day Today*. Dave Chappelle. Peter Kay. Jon Culshaw's impression of Dale Winton or Frank Bruno's laugh. All make me laugh out loud. So does Dominic. He made me laugh when he insulted the people of Norwich because they talk funny. Dom is from Norwich by the way – it's allowed. He also made me laugh when he and Dave formed their folk band Folkface. They would cover Kool and the Gang like you have never heard before. Their appearance at Glastonbury 2005 was legendary. Very very funny. Incidentally, the night before they played there, I happened to meet the actor who had just landed the part of Doctor Who, David Tennant. I can't remember how we met because I may have been a tad tipsy but I do remember him being lovely. Something tells me that Sophie introduced me to him, but she had never met him either so that doesn't really work. Anyway, David and I got chatting and I told him that I was on air from the site the next day with Vernon Kay. He asked if he could pop down and see us do the show (I might have actually invited *him*, I can't remember, but it sounds cooler if he asked to come and see us so that's how that story goes now) and I was more than happy.

The next day during the broadcast, a security guy comes to me and says, 'There's a David Tearnon to see you.'

Who the hell is David Tearnon? I've never heard of him. Unless he means Tennant.

OH SHIT! IT'S DOCTOR WHO!'

The slight recollection of meeting him the night before crossed my mind, and maybe I had told him to come down and say hello during the show. (I'm still sure he asked me.) We had planned, for the last half hour of the programme, to go out into the fields and find the jazz stage where Dave and Dom were performing as Folkface. We asked David Tennant if he fancied coming with us and he said yes. Now the Glastonbury festival is a big place. A very, very big place. Cut to half an hour later. There's me, Vernon Kay and David Tennant, the future travelling Time Lord, stood in the middle of a field, lost. An engineer, producer and about a hundred people surround us as we try and find a tent where a fake folk band is playing. To kill time, I asked David a knock-knock joke. He wasn't expecting it so I can officially say that I did his first ever knock-knock Doctor Who gag. How ace is that? He left shortly after explaining that he had to meet people. He never did see Folkface. He missed a treat.

Anyway, back to Dominic. Dom is a happily married man who has sparked some major discussions on the show. It was during a chat with him about his boy that I came out with something that slightly bemused him. We were talking about the lack of sleep he'd recently had (or not had – how does that work?). Anyway, Dom was telling me how little sleep he'd been getting because his son was very restless and kept crying and stuff. This prompted me to say that I'd rather have an iPod. To this day he has never let me forget that. Personally I don't get his point. Would you rather have a screaming, noisy, crying thing that puked and shat everywhere, or a state-of-the-art MP3 player that holds up to 8,000 songs? Exactly. Chris wins.

LONGMAN – SANDWICH KING

Now this is a strange one. Longman was a friend of a friend of mine. I was introduced to him by former Leeds United footballer Alan Smith. Al had known Longman for years and they were best pals. Every time I saw Al, I'd see Longman. After a while I'd see more of Longman than Alan. In fact, if I'm honest, Longman became my connection to Al, but now I speak to Longman most days of the week and only see Alan once in a while. Bloody footballers. Longman is named Longman as he is quite a tall fella. He's six foot five. His actual name is Benjamin. I found this out when I called him up one day only to get his answer phone message.

Hi, this is Benjamin. I'm not here right now. Please leave me a message.

When I finally got hold of him, I asked him the question:

'Who is Benjamin?'

What the hell was I thinking? I'd known him for twelve months and it never occurred to me that 'Longman' might not be his real name. Was I insane? How many Longman Smiths are there in the phone book?

Anyway, Longman has become a bit of a legend on our show. He opened up his own sandwich shop in Leeds and once in a while I would call him up and ask him what today's specials were. He'd reply with such classic lines as:

'Anyway, I've got to dash 'cos I'm going down cash 'n' carry to buy some beans.'

He put the Chris Moyles Chicken Curry sandwich on his specials board one week, and sold out.

He became an immediate hit with our listeners and has done some funny stuff on the show. He asked American rapper 50 Cent what his favourite sandwich filling is. His favourite to date, though, was when we were trying to get TV personality Angus Deayton on the show. We were playing a charity football match (well, I wasn't, obviously – I was managing) at West Ham's ground for the Soccer Six. It's an annual footy charity event for the music industry with two-bob celebrities playing football and raising money for some people or something, I'm not really sure. Anyway, Angus was playing in our team but proving difficult to get on air. So I decided to call Longman and pretend *he* was Angus Deayton instead. Despite not sounding anything like him whatsoever and almost getting us sued, it was a good job done. Longman was very proud.

Most listeners will have heard him being funny on air, but off air is another story. Longman loves a drink. Sometimes the drink doesn't love him back, but he loves a drink anyway. Longman is the only man I know who has urinated out of a convertible car. He's also the only man I know who's been kicked out of Disneyland for being drunk. Seriously, he was so pissed that Disney security threw him out. Amazingly, the embarrassment of being chucked out of Mickey Mouse's house didn't put him off, and he sneaked back in again. Only to have an experience that not many others have had:

DISNEY SECURITY THREW HIM OUT AGAIN!

Twice in one night. What a record. This gave rise to the famous song:

Oh Mickey Mouse
Won't let Longman in his house

which he sang, drunkenly, to me and Sophie one night in a hotel bar for two hours. What a legend.

His sandwich shop was originally called Wood Lane Stores, and had been so for years. Soon after he took over, he changed the name to Longman's, and put a big sign on the window. One day I was back in Leeds seeing the family so I called in. A car drove by and beeped its horn. Thinking it must be a mate of his, I asked who it was. Longman shrugged his shoulders. It happened again. Something wasn't right. Finally I asked him what was going on. 'People just beep,' he replied. People drive by the shop, see the sign and beep. It was happening several times a day. However, he then got very serious and said:

'Don't say owt on't radio, pal, 'cos if people start doing it all the time, the neighbours will complain.'

Brilliant. Here's a guy who has been forcibly removed from Disneyland for being shit-faced and he's worried about upsetting his neighbours! I still love the fella. He's a top mate.

ROB DJ – QUIZ HOST EXTRAORDINAIRE

Robert actually lives round the corner from my mum and dad in Leeds. I think I met him in the pub. I should remember, really, as it wasn't that long ago. We're now good mates. Rob had always wanted to be a DJ on the radio and was kind of a part-time local DJ anyway. During the day he has a proper job, but at night-time he turns into 'Rob DJ'. Complete with fake voice and an insane knowledge of music from the 1970s and 1980s, Rob DJ hosts the Monday-night quiz in my local in Leeds. I've only seen him do the quiz a few times as I work most Tuesday mornings 200 miles down the road in London. Or as Rob refers to it: 'Down in't smoke.' However, I did witness the quiz often enough to realise that we should do a pub quiz on the radio. Which is why, every Tuesday morning, we do 'Rob DJ's Monday Night Pub Quiz'. This consists of Rob doing the quiz as normal on a Monday night, then emailing the questions to our producer Rachel that evening. Rachel chooses five random questions that we play the following morning. Genius radio.

We've even taken Rob out on the road. He hosted a quiz for us one night in Sunderland in front of an invited audience. I met him in my local, and now he's a bloody star! The bizarre thing is that, just like the rest of the team, his fame is starting to affect him. I put these people on air because I think they'll be funny or give the audience a laugh. Since doing the quiz, Rob has been recognised in New York, signs autographs and, the last time I saw him, told me he wants to write his very own Rob DJ quiz book. The bloke's an electrician from Leeds, for Christ's sake!

CARRIE DAVIES – THE QUEEN OF SPORT

When I was choosing the team to work with me on the breakfast show, I originally picked a woman called Juliette to be the sport girl. I love the idea of a girl talking sport all morning. Most sport readers on the radio are men so it's a nice change, plus I think it makes sport more accessible when a woman reads it. Juliette had occasionally read for us before when we presented the afternoon show, but now I had a chance to have her every day (if you'll pardon the expression). She was brilliant. Bright, sassy, an amazing knowledge of football and she had great breasts – everything I needed in my sport journalist. So the team was in place and I was very happy. Everything was going swimmingly. (By the way, what does that expression mean exactly? Personally I find swimming leaves me cold, wet and tired.) The show was getting good results both with the audience and the critics. Then, after only about six months, a bombshell:

JULIETTE DECIDED SHE WANTED TO LEAVE.

Turns out that Jules was getting fed up with her London life and decided she'd be better off leaving the show and moving back up North to a job on Radio Five Live. I was proper gutted. My ideal line-up had collapsed in less than a year and we had to find a replacement for somebody I thought was perfect. She was hilarious after a couple of drinks and was even known to do the splits in public. Luckily Rod McKenzie, the head of

Radio 1 *Newsbeat*, came to the rescue and provided us with a list of possible replacements. I looked at the list. It had one name on it.

'Seriously, we need to find somebody brilliant – we can't just have a list of one,' I screamed at Ben Cooper.

'I agree it's not a long list,' Ben said.

'Not a long list? I could write a longer list of women I've slept with, and that's saying something!'

We explained to Rod that we needed to try a few people out and asked him to extend the list. This he did, with a list of people I genuinely believe he knew were crap. First on the list was a girl with so little experience she didn't even have a demo tape. Second was a girl who, in spite of her quite strong speech impediment *and* lisp, was perfect. No thank you. We listened to all the tapes of the women on the list until we got to the original name Rod had given us. The woman's name was Carrie Davies and, despite having a name that made her sound like the ex-Radio 1 legendary DJ Gary Davies, it turned out that Rod hadn't done that badly. To make things even better, she was blonde, had a nice figure and, just like Jules:

CARRIE HAD LARGE BREASTS AS WELL.

Now before you go thinking I'm being all sexiest, I'm not. When you work at such a ridiculous time of the morning, you take any perk you can. I've even got excited when Aled's given me a hug at 6.30 in the morning. We invited Carrie to come on a night out with us in Birmingham to see if we bonded. She turned up to the bar looking gorgeous, seemed comfortable and relaxed with us and, best of all, was dancing on a table within about ninety minutes. Carrie was perfect for the job.

She does, though, have some weird little tendencies. The worst one being that she is the most ticklish person I have *ever* met. If you go anywhere near her, and trust me I've tried, then she does this kind of spasm thing and shrieks like a monkey. If you manage to make contact and actually tickle her, she will more often than not, and I swear this is true, end up in a ball on the floor. And this is after a little jab tickle, not a proper get-stuck-in tickle. It is one of the funniest things we have seen, and after two years of working together it still hasn't lost any comedy value at all. Even Rachel tickles her at least once a week. It's a nice release and always makes you smile. Granted, I don't think Carrie sees it that way, but what can you do?

I really like Carrie. She's funny, posh and knows her sport. She's also cute with nice breasts and makes me look like I hang out with good-looking people, when in real life I don't. This is emphasised in the fact that Carrie has never taken me out socially or introduced me to any of her friends.

5

LEEDS UNITED

Don't worry if you're not into football, I won't go on!

Let me finally sort this issue out once and for all. When I was younger my family had an affinity with Leeds United Football Club. In those days the supporters' club was next to the ground and the training pitch sat right behind it. I remember the club shop, a kind of hut next to the supporters' club, and I remember going to the ground both for the odd game and to take a look when it was all empty one day. I also remembered that I had no interest in football **WHATSOEVER**. It just wasn't the kind of thing that me or my brother liked. I didn't play, I didn't really watch. I just wasn't a big football fan.

Cut straight to 1996 when I started working in London. I'd jump in a taxi and the driver would notice my northern accent.

'Where you from, mate?' the cabbie would ask.

'Leeds, pal,' I'd reply.

'Oh, dirty Leeds, eh? Elland Road. I've been up there a few times. Remember the game against Fulham, Christmas 1985?'

'Not really, mate. I'm not actually a—' I wouldn't be able to finish my words.

'We'd beaten you at our place 3–1 but then you did us with a great goal from, oh, what's his name again? Oh yeah, Sheridan.'

'As I said, I'm not really a fan of—'

'Yeah yeah. Dirty Leeds, eh? Remember Terry Cooper. Now he was a player. Scored against the arse, didn't he. Love that. Did it twice in fact in both the FA cup and ...'

At this point I give up and gently drift off. It really was odd. Every time a bloke heard I was from Leeds, they would assume I was a Leeds United fan. At the same time I had started talking about the city of Leeds a lot on the radio show. When I joined Radio 1 it was very London-biased, so a few Leeds mentions would be a refreshing change. Once I spoke about Leeds the place, again people assumed I was a Leeds United fan. It got worse.

'April 2000. Ian Harte hacked Dennis Bergkamp down. Remember that?'

'Not really pal, I'm not a—'

'Your lot went mental saying that Bergkamp dived, but I was there, it was definitely—'

I DON'T GIVE A FUCKING SHITE. SHUT THE FUCK UP!

(For the record, it was a dive!)

So I was getting myself a reputation for being a Leeds United fan. I began to get invites to the London games from various Leeds fans who worked in the record industry. By this point, I decided to give in and go to a few games. Surprisingly, I loved it. I really did. Apart from the result most of the time, but I found myself getting sucked in by the whole atmosphere. I ended up getting tickets for Elland Road and, before I knew it, I was going to games with my dad, a little later than he was hoping, as I was twenty-seven years old and not twelve.

Coincidentally, my friend Simon Ross left London to go and work at my old stomping ground Radio Aire. He immediately ingratiated himself into the Leeds lifestyle and within a few weeks knew all the bar owners and hotel managers. It was from a night out that I met a few of the Leeds players.

Dominic Matteo was the first player I met (if you exclude Billy Bremner, who lived down the road from Mum and Dad's). Dominic was very tall and extremely polite and likeable. By this time I had decided to get some season tickets for Dad and me. Dom helped me get some decent seats and then stalled for weeks over the payment.

'Get it, pal. You're not paying for them. My treat,' he said.

How cool was that? My season tickets for Leeds were given to me by the future captain of the club! After I met Dom, I went on to meet a few more players. It was a very exciting time for me. I has just got into the Leeds thing and now found myself standing with the players after a game on a Saturday night. Now I know a lot of die-hard football fans say that unless you support your team from the time you can walk, you're not a proper fan. If you come into football later in life, it's just a fad. If you live away from your club and don't go to all the home matches, you're just a fickle supporter. Well, if you're thinking any of those things:

I COULDN'T GIVE A SHIT!

I am the complete opposite of a 'glory hunter'. As my interest in Leeds United kicked in, they were pretty much just falling out of Europe, having reached the semi-final of the Champions League but losing 3–0 to Valencia. Just a few years later and there I am watching us draw 0–0 with Stoke. And I'm still a fan. Despite them being a bit rubbish and playing without the quality of a few years ago, I'm still hanging in there. So I don't really care that I'm not a 'proper' fan.

Right, rant over. Here are just a few of the players I met when we were still playing in the Premiership.

Alan Smith was a brilliant player and a very funny man. I met him at his twenty-first birthday party in Leeds, which I somehow managed to blag my way into. Alan has one of the broadest Leeds accents ever. It is *so* strong. His tone doesn't change either. Sometimes it's hard to work out whether he's happy or pissed off. Unlike some footballers, Al doesn't drink alcohol. Instead he will sit down with you and have a pot of tea. One night we were drinking in the bar of the Malmaison Hotel in Leeds when I decided that I was going to drink tea just like my good friend Alan. I ordered two pots of tea, one for me and one for him. He was very pleased that I had decided to join him in his non-alcoholic drinking session and he was even more impressed when I ordered another, and then another.

'Why the hell are you drinking tea?' asked one of my mates.

'Leave him alone. If he wants to drink tea, then he can drink tea,' said Alan.

I didn't have the heart to tell him that for the past four rounds I had asked the barman to pour two bottles of Miller into each teapot for me. Alan hadn't noticed a thing, even when my tea looked slightly frothier than his.

Eirik Bakke was introduced to me one Saturday night. I'd love to tell you what he said to me, but with Eirik, I never actually understood a word. His strong Norwegian accent is ridiculous. He sounds like some bizarre foreign cartoon character. Eirik is a very nice fella, though. He is also very professional, and the following story took place during a time when no football was on.

I'm a simple man when it comes to drink. Lager is my thing and I'm not really into shorts or spirits. One night in a bar, Eirik decided to order sambuca. He bought about twelve shots and carried them back to our table on a tray. Eirik had been relaxing that evening taking a well-earned break from football, and therefore had enjoyed a few drinks. I'm not sure how many he'd had, but by the time he reached our table with his tray of twelve shot glasses, he had spilt so many that only four were left upright.

Rio Ferdinand is a huge bloke. I only met him a couple of times but he was considered to be very stylish and one night out wore the biggest tie I had ever seen. You know the knot bit of the tie? Well, Rio's was about the same size as my head. Fashion and footballers don't always go together.

Michael Bridges was, for a brief period, my dad's favourite player at Leeds United. I went to the official shop next to the ground one day to buy a few shirts and Dad decided to get one with Bridgey's name on the back. 'I don't know what squad number he'll be this season,' said the girl behind the counter. So Dad ended up with a shirt with no number on the back, but *BRIDGES* written across the top.

Now a lot of footballers get a bad reputation for being wild party animals when they're off the pitch. Bridgey called me one afternoon when I was on Radio 1 and said that he and his mum were listening to the show ... as they played Scrabble. He's so rock 'n' roll. Nice one, pal.

Harry Kewell was one of my favourite players at Leeds. On the pitch, if he was in right mood, he was outstanding. And it turned out that as much as I loved him, he loved my radio show. He didn't come out with the other lads as often as he was married with a couple of kids, but he did turn up to my birthday drinks one year. I didn't know he had been invited, and when he walked through the door I was so excited I must have looked like a young girl at a Justin Timberlake concert. I've met many famous people, but for some reason I become a small child the few times I've been in his company. I was gutted when he left us for Liverpool.

Paul Robinson was the Leeds United goalkeeper and is not the man in *Neighbours* played by Stefan Dennis. I first met him in February 2003 when he played his first game for England as a second-half substitute in a friendly against Australia. After the game he gave me an England shirt signed by all the team.

'Are you sure you want to give me this? It's your first England game,' I said.

'Yeah, it 's all right. Keep it,' he replied.

I did, and I still have it. The deal was he would get me tickets for the game if I was the DJ at his wedding. Playing DJ at the wedding of the future England number one sounded like a good deal to me. (I never did DJ at his wedding in the end, but I did enjoy lots of drinks!) Paul and I have remained good friends and now that he plays for Spurs I see more of him as he lives nearer.

Paul and I have a gag that goes back to when I used to play Fifa Football on the Xbox. When Leeds scored a goal, Paul's computer image would shrug his shoulders up and down in a sort of monkey way. This led to me call Paul 'Monkey Man'. One time Sophie and I went to see him play at White Hart Lane. We sat in his box, which has a perfect view of Paul on the goal line. Seconds before the game kicked off, Paul looked over to the box and, knowing I was in there, gave me the Monkey Man shoulder shrug. This to us was very funny, and I would have loved the cameras to pick it up as some sort of weird warm-up. I'm just glad he didn't see me watching him play in the World Cup and give me the shrug there, 'cos that would have been embarrassing.

Sadly most of the players I knew have since left the club and it's a different time now, but I'll still go on supporting Leeds. And I'll be there when we get back into the Premiership.

5

7

5
HOSPITAL RADIO

t must have been my absolute addiction to the idea of being on the radio for a living that brought me to the wonderful world of hospital radio. For people outside of the UK, and for those who just don't know what it is, hospital radio is a radio station, inside a hospital, broadcasting to the patients of the hospital. Genius. When I was looking to learn my craft, which basically means sitting in a studio talking to yourself and playing records, I found it very difficult to be taken seriously. Nobody would give me a break. Nobody would hire me. Nobody said to me:

'Hey there, young fella. Why not come and be on the radio at our station? Play around with the equipment and get yourself some experience.'

They didn't say that to me, because I was twelve years old. I admit that was very young to be saying to radio stations that I wanted some work, but I was twelve and I didn't know any better. Looking back it does amaze me that I got *anybody* to take me even remotely seriously, as I couldn't drive, drink or grow any facial hair (that didn't happen for at least another eighteen months). But at that age you don't think like an adult. Not once did I think I might be too young. I knew I was young, not even a teenager, but I wanted to do radio and thought somebody would help me out. Eventually somebody did. They told me that I should try the hospital radio station they worked at. It was in Wakefield, about a twenty-minute drive from my house (I know that because Mum would drive me there).

Unlike the traditional hospital radio stations, this one didn't just broadcast to the hospital it was based in. It broadcast to four hospitals. It was networked! I imagined the countless beds of sick people, so ill they didn't have the energy to switch the damn thing off. A captive audience. As it turned out, I think most were so ill they didn't have the energy to turn it *on*. There was also another slight problem. Maybe problem is the wrong word. A slight hitch perhaps. The kind of hitch that prevents you from popping down to the wards and collecting requests. The hitch was that this particular hospital radio studio ...

WAS BASED IN A MENTAL HOSPITAL!

Now, remember it did broadcast to three other hospitals, one of them being the home of a renowned burns unit. It just also happened to be home to many mentally unstable people who thought they were Mars Bars or king of the planet Zuntar.

Nevertheless, it was a hospital radio station that was pleased for me to go and visit. They were willing to give me a chance. So I took it. With both hands, and an eye on the fella shaking in the corner who kept shouting out random words at the top of his voice.

WBHS in Wakefield would be my first radio home. Not proper radio. Not a paid job. But somewhere I could play and learn and have a hell of a lot of fun.

It turned out to be a sort of playground for me and several other young wannabe radio DJs. Every Saturday afternoon, my mum would take me and drop me off just outside a side entrance to Stanley Royd Hospital. Once inside, I took a quick left and went up the stairs. If there happened to be a patient sitting on the stairs, we were told to ignore them because they weren't doing any harm. At the age of thirteen, as I was by then, some clinically insane person rocking back and forth while humming what sounded like 'Jingle Bells' was not going to put me off. I had dreams. I had ideas. I had a fill-in spot for Adrian who did the oldies show.

This was it. The beginning of my radio career. In a mental hospital. Surrounded by insane people.

I met many cool people at WBHS. Dave Parker was the coolest. He was the programme controller. Funny, really, how seriously we all took it. We had jingles. We had two studios. We went twenty-four hours a day while I was there. Yet none of us could be bothered to go and collect requests or talk to the patients. And why should we. Fuck 'em. Who cares about them?

I'M ON THE RADIO NOW!

Dave Parker was good to me. He knew I wanted to learn about radio. He also saw that even at the age of thirteen, I had some skill. I knew about hitting the vocal of a record. I knew about timing and was good on the equipment. He put me on air and taught me lots about presenting. We also had a lot of laughs. At the start of our second year of the breakfast show on Radio 1, I met him again, at a Q&A I did in Leeds. At the end of it I had to give out an award to a small station. The boss of the station came up to receive the award. It was Dave Parker. Still doing the radio, but this time with fewer mental people. I hope. Thanks for the start, Dave.

Anyway, back to hospital radio. The fact that there were many unstable patients around was never a worry for the thirteen-year-old Chris Moyles. They were almost invisible after a while. Occasionally you would have to step over one of them on your way to the toilet, but apart from that you didn't really notice them. I only heard one funny story about the 'unusual audience' we had.

One of the DJs was on air, sitting in Studio 1. To get to the station, you had to climb these *five* flights of big, hard hospital steps. At the top was a door. It had a security combination push-button thing and one of those frosted-glass windows. From the inside you could see if someone was on the other side of the glass, but you couldn't make out if it was a man, woman or child. The DJ noticed what looked like a man out there and went and opened the door.

'Hi. Can I help you?' asked the DJ.

'Yeah. I'm doing a show,' replied the man.

'Oh, you're the new guy. Nice to meet you.'

They swapped pleasantries and Mr On-air DJ showed Mr New DJ where the coffee machine was and where the papers were, etc.

'Records are through there. Choose whatever you want to play and I'll see you back in the studio.'

The new DJ went to the record library next to the studio and started going through the songs. One by one he took the records out. Looked at them. Then threw each one across the room like a frisbee. Song by song, disc by disc, they flew through the air, smashing on contact with the studio window.

It was at this point that Mr On-air DJ received a call from the guy on after him saying that he would be a little late for his show as he was stuck in traffic.

The first mental person I ever heard of who thought he was a DJ. He wouldn't, however, be my last.

This industry is full of mental people.

MY FAVOURITE GUESTS

DAVINA McCALL

I've always liked Davina McCall. I think most people do. A lot of my
friends have asked me what she's like in real life. The truth is, she's a
pain in the arse. Only joking. She is as lovely as she is on television.
She's as funny and as sweet. She's the kind of woman that girls want to
be and blokes want to marry. Her husband is a very lucky man. He likes a
drink and she doesn't drink. But she still absolutely loves him. Lucky
bastard. How many men get grief from their other halves for drinking?
At some time or other, pretty much all of us, right? Not him. Here's a
man who's good-looking, charming and married to Davina McBloodyCall.
He's on the couch watching the rugby and having a few beers, and she
doesn't care. In fact, she's quite happy to let him lie there because he
likes the rugby! Here's a woman who doesn't drink and who is so in

love with her husband that if he wants a few beers with the boys it doesn't matter.

I GET GRIEF FOR GOING TO MY LOCAL TOO OFTEN!

As I said, he's a lucky man.

I first spoke to Davina on the radio show on Radio 1 when we did afternoons. Dale Winton was our guest that day, I believe, and she phoned in to say hello to him. She came on air and was like:

'I love you guys. I can't believe I'm talking to Chris Moyles.'

'We've been trying to get you on the show for the last twelve months but you won't come on it,' I yelled.

'I'll come on your show any time. I'd love to,' she replied.

Off the air I thanked her for phoning and explained that I was telling the truth. In this wonderful, ridiculous world of entertainment and showbiz bollocks, you mostly have to go through an agent to get somebody on the show which can be difficult. 'Not available at the moment' is one reply. 'They're not doing any press at the moment' is another, and then you see them the next day on GMTV, probably because they're getting paid for it. Agents do my head in. They take a percentage of your money and scratch their arse while doing so. Of course, my agent is different. Although, as if to prove she's from the same family, she does have similar traits. For example, I know she won't read this book until the deal is done. Seventy thousand words is way too much to read when you're busy counting *my money*! Still, she does have large breasts and is actually quite sweet.

Sorry, I went on a bit of a rant there. Back to Davina.

So after Davina had spoken to us and given us the green light to get her any time, we called her agent. Eventually she did come on the show. She bounced into the studio like Tigger. She was so excited about meeting us all and being on the show with us. She's been on several times since and she still gets excited each time she comes in, which is great. And I've seen her bottom. I have such a great job.

Here's another reason why I love her. Every year I get a phone call. A giddy voice at the end will whisper down the line:

'Guess what I can see right now?'

I know what the call is as soon as I've heard those words. It means Davina has turned up at work for rehearsals and is looking at the new Big Brother house! She gets as worked up about the show as the rest of us nutters who love it. We speak a lot during the series and then she disappears out of my life for another few months, although these days I do know she listens to the show most mornings driving her children to school. Bless her.

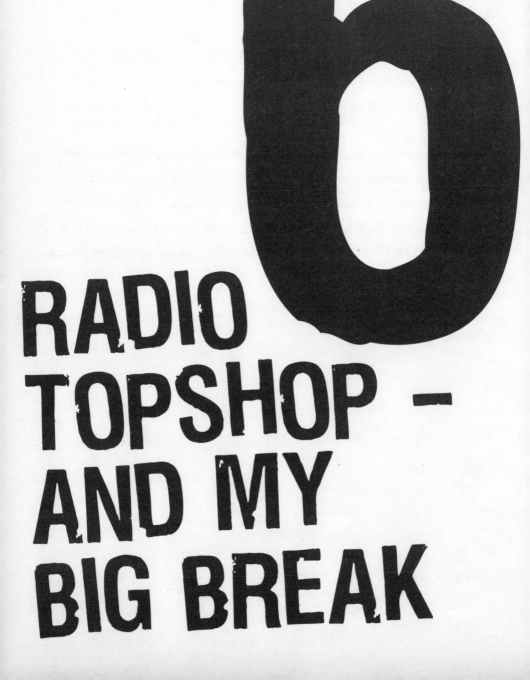

6

RADIO TOPSHOP – AND MY BIG BREAK

So there I was, a thirteen-year-old chubby kid from Leeds who dreamt of being a big-time disc jockey. I had found hospital radio, now I just needed to make the next big step. Somehow I had to go from schoolboy to radio star. I knew this wasn't going to be easy. Nobody in my family was remotely connected with show business. My mum always told us that she had been on camera – Irish dancing on the first ever night of RTE Television in Ireland – but that was like fifty years ago. Besides, I don't think lifting my knees up and down while dressed as a leprechaun is going to get me to the BBC. After writing to lots of radio stations and asking them for a job, then getting the usual bog-standard 'Go away, silly' replies, I knew I had to try elsewhere. Then two amazing things happened at once. One slightly greater than the other, but they both turned out to be turning points in my route to radio stardom. First, a guy called Carl Kingston called me and changed my life for ever.

Carl was the evening-show presenter for my local independent station in Leeds, Radio Aire. At that time, local radio stations really thought they ought to be local, so lots of them were named after the local river, so ours was Radio Aire. I always thought how funny it would've been if a city had the river Shite flowing through it. You can just hear the jingles now.

'All your favourite music, here on Radio Shite!'

Anyway, Carl did the evening show, seven to ten each weekday night. He was ace. He was very straight, but a brilliant DJ. I had bugged him to let me help him out on his evening radio show, and eventually he said yes! This was it. I would be hanging out with loads of great DJs and then one day the boss would stick me on air and I'd officially be a DJ myself. Actually, that's not a million miles away from the truth, except that some of the DJs at Radio Aire were rubbish and horrible people, and it took me a few years of making tea and working for free before anything happened – but more on that later.

The second thing that happened to me was in-store radio. In-store radio is exactly what it says. A radio station in a shop, which broadcasts to the shop. In this case it was Topshop and Top Man, in Briggate, in Leeds city centre. They had a studio downstairs in the basement, right in the middle of the knickers and bras section. My kind of studio. I went to visit the DJ there one day, a guy by the name of Brian Kirby. He was kind enough to make me some jingles and showed me how it all worked. Nice guy. About eighteen months later I popped back into the store. They had moved the studio from the basement to the ground floor. It stood on three huge pillar-type legs and looked out over the whole floor. It wasn't a million miles away from the alien spaceships in *The War of the Worlds*, only it was a studio with no air-conditioning, and overlooked the women's changing rooms. I climbed the virtually vertical staircase and knocked on the door. Brian was still there and even remembered me from before. We got chatting again and I told him of my hospital radio stuff and the local Radio Aire work. (Hardly work, making tea and sending out prizes, but it was a start.) He told me to pop back in the week when his boss would be visiting from Manchester. I did. It was a Thursday night, leading up to Christmas. Peter Knott was his name, and he talked to me for all of fifteen minutes before turning round and saying:

'Right then, young lad. Let's see what you sound like.'

He gave me fifteen minutes to have a go, while he walked round the store and listened to see if I was any good. Brilliant. A live audition. I could easily do this. So I sat down at the tiny mixing desk and worked my magic. Or at least what magic you can work in a studio that broadcasts to three floors of shoppers on a Thursday night.

Well, I must have been good, 'cos the guy didn't come back for almost an hour. He must have been blown away by my radio skill at such a young age. Either that or he popped out to the Ship up the road for a pint or two. When he came back, he said he was impressed and pretty much offered me a job there on the spot. It was a strange kind of job, but I wasn't complaining. It turned out that the DJ Brian Kirby had a season ticket for Leeds United and was moaning that he was always missing games because he had to work Saturday afternoons. Enter schoolboy DJ Moyles. I was offered the job of doing every other Saturday afternoon from about 2 o'clock until closing. I'd done it. My first paid radio job, once a fortnight,

FROM AN OVERHEATED STUDIO OVERLOOKING THE LADIES' FITTING ROOMS OF TOPSHOP!

Who the fuck cared? I was living my dream. Plus I got 15 per cent discount on all the silk shirts and waistcoats I could find in Top Man ... well, it was 1989.

Radio Topshop was great fun. Every other Saturday I'd turn up, all excited. Brian would be all excited too because he was off to see Leeds play. The older girls on the shop floor thought I was cute, and the younger ones liked me because I played records for them if they asked me to. It was all going really well. Until something terrible happened.

BRIAN RESIGNED.

Now this should have been a good thing. But it wasn't. I was offered the job straight away, and I said I wanted to take it, but it was about February and I had my GCSE exams to do first.

'Not a problem,' said Peter, the boss. 'We'll just get somebody else to fill in.'

I told them I'd do it, but after I'd done my exams and also taken a little holiday. Even back then I knew holidays were important! I said I wanted my six weeks in the summer but would start after that. Peter agreed. I was due to start the same week that my other mates would start college. Brilliant.

'Just one thing,' I said to Peter.

'Yeah, sure.'

'Where are you going to find a DJ to fill in for a sixteen-year-old schoolboy until he's done his exams and can take the job on?'

Peter looked at me, and with a dead straight face told me: **'We won't tell 'em!'**

Cool! How great was that. I'd have my own fill-in, but he wouldn't know about it. How funny would that be? Answer: not very funny at all. Enter Mr DJ Fill-in. This was the man who would almost make me quit radio before I had even properly started. He was a few years older than me, and I hated him. For some strange reason, I kept the Saturday afternoon thing, although they made it weekly rather than every Leeds United home game. I knew this was to keep me happy until I took the job on full-time. Mr DJ Fill-in, who had no idea of the true situation, told me it was because he didn't want to work Saturday afternoons. This is what I put up with: FOR SIX MONTHS!

Anyway, eventually my time came and he disappeared. I had only worked there full-time for one month, while still helping out at Radio Aire, when my official big break came.

At that time, 1990, radio stations were tight with money. (Not much has changed.) An overnight sustaining service was set up called Radio Radio. This service would broadcast from ten at night until six the following morning. It meant that instead of each radio station hiring two or three DJs to do the night-time shows, they all just put this service out on the air and let it run itself. It had DJs like Jonathan Ross on there and odd people like Ruby Wax, in the days when she was funny. Then it changed hands and turned into the 'Super Station'. Still the same idea but with other DJs.

All I remember is being in Radio Aire one night, when one of the DJs, Mike Vittie, told me that the service had gone bust or something and was due to close within the next twenty-four hours. Suddenly, all these local radio stations would need night-time DJs. He told me to get my arse into the studio the next day and tell the boss I'd do a show for £25. So I did. The night before, my dad helped me work out a big speech, explaining that I wanted to prove myself and that I knew I could be an asset to the radio station. I went in and hovered around the boss's office. He saw me hovering and called me in for a chat. He explained to me that he needed DJs straight away, and would I be prepared to do a show that night, for £30. I told him of course I would, but I'd have trouble getting in as I was sixteen years old and couldn't drive.

'How much is a taxi gonna be?' he asked.

'About £4.50,' I said.

'In that case, call it £30 a shift and £9 taxi expenses.'

I couldn't believe it. I'd got a job and a £14 rise and hadn't even delivered any of my prepared speech.

'Now, what did you want to see me about anyway?' he asked.

'Nothing. It can wait.'

> **I had finally got my first show on the radio. I was sixteen years old and was going to get paid £39 for doing it. They were going to pay me for doing what I had always wanted to do.**

A few of the DJs there were really pleased for me. Some of the rest, sadly, were a bunch of egomaniacs who felt threatened by a fucking sixteen-year-old, for Christ's sake. Kenny Stevens, a really nice Scottish guy, was pleased for me. As too was Mike Vittie, who had a really fit girlfriend too. Carl Kingston, my mentor, was pleased also. He remains pleased and proud of me to this day. For a few years I tried to acknowledge him in interviews for his influence on my career. It always seemed to get chopped out in favour of me slagging someone famous off. So finally I get to say it here. Thank you, Carl, for helping me out, and letting me work my nuts off for you, for free, and for several years too, you cheap bastard! You're one of the best, and I promise not to tell anybody about your favourite trick of asking prostitutes for directions when I travelled with you on gigs and then adding: 'What about the lad? It's his first time.' It scarred me for life. Thanks, pal.

I was working at Radio Topshop during the day, and then doing Radio Aire at the weekends with the occasional fill-in during the week. I was on the radio, for God's sake, and the real radio for that matter. No more mentally sick people for me, now I had people in cars or on building sites – what a dream come true.

I'd get into Topshop for about 10.15 a.m. I normally started at eleven, but I had to record the last thirty minutes of the day onto tape in order to get the bus, or run if the bus was late, down the road to the Radio Aire studios. It was hardly limousine action. I think I was the only DJ on Radio Aire who got the number 63 bus down to Kirkstall Road and legged it down the drive to the studios to do a show, arriving all hot and sticky.

THE RADIO TOPSHOP FORMAT

Bizarrely, even though Radio Topshop just broadcast through some speakers to a shop, the management team who ran the stations had a strict format to follow. It was the funniest thing ever. As far I remember it ran something like this:

11 a.m. OPEN THE STATION

What they meant was: switch the power on and play a record.

12 p.m. THE GOLDEN HOUR

The same as Simon Bates used to do, but to a shop.

1 p.m. CHART SOUNDS

Do me a favour. It was starting to sound like the reviews on Ceefax. My favourite bit of the day though was:

5 p.m. LOVE SONGS

Who the fuck is getting amorous in Topshop at five in the afternoon?

5.15 p.m. READ OUT TONIGHT'S TV LISTINGS

I swear this was true. What a waste of time.

5.20 p.m. ANNOUNCE THAT THE STORE WILL CLOSE IN TEN MINUTES. ANYBODY WISHING TO MAKE A PURCHASE SHOULD PROCEED TO THE TILLS NOW

In other words – please buy whatever it is you're thinking about, we're desperate for your cash.

5.30 p.m. CLOSE DOWN THE STATION

I.e. switch the power off and piss off home.

Even at that early age, and without that much radio experience, I knew that this format was absolute bollocks. So what did I do? Did I try to explain to the RTS management team that this format didn't really suit the young shoppers that Topshop was attracting? Did I balls. I just ignored it and played what the hell I wanted to. Remember, shoppers were in and out in an average of fifteen minutes. The staff, however, worked there all day. So I played them whatever they wanted to hear. And it worked. So much so that if the guys in Top Man upstairs jumped hard enough in the right bit of the floor, the vibration would rock the studio underneath and the CD would jump. Oh, how they loved their little jokes. Fucking shirt-sellers!

Anyway, back to the story. I would record the last thirty minutes onto tape and ask one of the kind girls on the shop floor, Carol or Angie the fit one with the big boobs, to switch the studio off after the tape ran out. Speaking of Angie, she was a really cute girl, married to a really good-looking guy.

They were like the Posh and Becks of Topshop and Top Man in Leeds. She had done some modelling and asked me once if she should enter a *Daily Sport* topless model competition. Well, who was I to shatter her dreams of being a topless model? I immediately said yes and off she went. I had forgotten all about it when one day one of the guys from upstairs in Top Man was sitting in the staff room reading a copy of the *Daily Sport*. They were a very classy crowd there, you know. He started freaking out – 'cos Angie was in the paper … with no top on! Scandalous. Because I was young and naïve, or stupid even, I never looked at the picture because I knew her and thought it would be weird. What a poof. I don't know what I was thinking of, because even to this day I'd love to see her breasts.

Where was I? Oh yeah, tape. So I'd stick the pre-recorded half-hour on and rush out of the store and down the road to Radio Aire. In those days they used to do the catchily titled 'Non-stop Top Twenty' every night between six and seven. On a Monday you would record it live, playing songs from number twenty to number one. On a Tuesday you'd do the same thing but from number one to number twenty. Then on Wednesday you would play Monday's tape, on Thursday you would play Tuesday's tape … you get the idea.

The afternoon DJ at that time was the really nice Scottish guy called Kenny Stevens. (I have a theory that to be a real DJ, your surname has to be a Christian name with an added S. Such as Tony Johns, John Simons, Mike James, etc.) Now it's fair to say that Kenny Stevens wasn't the tidiest DJ I had ever met. He would get his records out from the shelves behind him in the studio, play them on air, put the record back in the sleeve and toss it over his shoulder. I would arrive in the studio at 5.58 p.m. every weekday. But on the Monday and the Tuesday I had until the end of the news at 6.03 to wind the big reel-to-reel tape onto the big reel-to-reel machine, get the

Non-stop Top Twenty jingles out of the rack and find the first few records, which would be somewhere on the floor of the studio, in among the other thirty records.

'Kenny, where the hell is "Love Is All Around" by Wet Wet Wet?'

'Erm, I played that in the second hour, I think, so it'll be over near the bin.'

Sure enough, there I'd find it.

'Did you play Roxette?'

'Erm, yeah. First hour. Over to the left near the chair.'

Every Monday and Tuesday night I had to spend the first twenty minutes crawling around the studio floor on my hands and knees looking for records. I'd play the first record in full while looking for the second. Then I'd play all the second song while looking for the third. I spent so much time looking for songs on the floor that I didn't time any of the records properly. By the time I was playing the fourth record it was about twenty past six. That meant that I had forty minutes to play another sixteen records before seven o'clock. So when I did the 'Non-stop Top Twenty' it ended up being the 'Non-stop Top Fifteen'. The best thing was:

NOBODY EVER NOTICED!

He was always nice to me, though, Kenny, and even helped me make a demo tape so I could move on. His idea was to make it less than a minute long, as a bit of a novelty.

'By the time the kettle is boiled you will have decided what you think of me,' was the tacky line on the letter. It worked: I got a reaction from Radio 1 saying, **'You're right. I knew by the time the kettle boiled that your tape was too short!'**

There were two bosses at Radio Aire: the managing director and the programme controller. Now it seemed to me that the managing director's job was to completely ignore the DJs in the corridor as he walked to the sales area to find out how much money his sales team were making him. I remember the joy of walking around the building, so proud that I was now a real DJ on my local radio station. The managing director would walk down the corridor on his way to visit the sales people.

'Morning, sir,' I'd politely say.

Silence would be his response.

Charming. I'm working my balls off for him trying to sound as good as I could, and he can't even be arsed to say hello. It wasn't just me who felt this way. One of the station's established DJs used to joke with me about him too. He got the same treatment, but he found it amusing. He was shocked one day when the MD said hello back. He thought he must have mistaken him for one of the sales guys. The worst bit of all was one Christmas when the MD held an open house for staff to pop in and have a drink with him and his family. I had no intention of going, but my mum was adamant that I should. With my whole family. To show that I was a good team player.

WHAT A FUCKING MISTAKE THAT WAS.

I turned up with my mum and dad in tow. Remember, I was still a sixteen-year-old boy fresh from doing his GCSE exams. I rang the bell, and a few moments later he opened the door. I can't even begin to imagine what was going through his mind. In front of him were a chubby schoolboy, a balding postman in his fifties and a small Irish woman who looked rather like a pale Oompa-Loompa. It was the most uncomfortable hour of my life. When he opened the door, I don't believe he had a clue who I was.

I half expected him to say hello to my dad first, thinking that he must be one of the oldies station DJs.

The programme controller was different. He *did* speak to me. I suppose I'm grateful to him because technically he gave me my first proper radio gig. However, it wasn't like he was some football scout who had been keeping an eager eye on me for a while. I had worked there making tea and looking after guests for free for about two years. Also, once I had the job, I was fighting a losing battle to try and keep the damn thing. I spent a lot of time at Radio Aire just trying to hold on to my on-air shifts. The programme controller had hired another young DJ, by the name of Nick Babb (you can tell that was his real name) and was constantly taking me off a show and putting Nick on.

Now just in case you were thinking that it could have been that Babb was better than me – he wasn't. No offence to the guy, I mean I was hardly Terry Wogan at that age, but I did have, if I say so myself, an amazing amount of skill for a recent ex-schoolboy. He, on the other hand, ran mobile discos, and had the surname Babb. I rest my case. The programme controller gave me the Saturday night show, then took it off me, 'cos he thought people wanted to listen to love songs on a Saturday night and I wasn't the love-songs type. I agree with the last bit, I wasn't. But love songs on a Saturday night? Do me a favour. Love-song shows on the radio are *always* aimed at couples who are in love and lying in bed in each other's arms on a Saturday night listening to all the lovely love songs together.

BOLLOCKS.

If you're the kind of person who likes listening to love songs on the radio and you're in on a Saturday night:

YOU'RE SINGLE!

And what the hell are you doing lying on your own listening to songs about happy couples for? Maybe finding a partner is the thing you should be doing on a Saturday night. Or hanging outside the local shops acting weird!

The next move, after I'd been DJing for about six months, was filling in for my mentor Carl Kingston. I got that gig, and worked hard to do a good job. This was the show I'd helped out on for years so I knew the format inside out. Once again, the controller decided to give Babb a go. He ran the station like a parent dishing out toys to young children.

'Now come on, Chris, you did it for three weeks. Let the other DJs have a go.'

The late-night slot at that time was held by a guy called Tony Adams. Not the footballer, by the way, in case you're stupid and think that he was also a part-time DJ. This Tony Adams was a strange kind of a fellow. I never realised just how strange he was until I worked with him later at Radio Luxembourg, but that's for another story. Tony, it had to be said, had *the* most complicated late-night show on radio in the world *ever*. Complicated feature after complicated feature. The guy was always doing a chart from ten years ago with clips and news stories from that particular second, or a quiz with songs edited together and you had to tell him what the B-sides were or something like that. I filled on that show once, and the notes he gave on all the features read like a NASA manual. I never did that show again either.

Eventually I was reduced to doing one overnight show a week, Sunday night into Monday morning, 1 a.m. to 6 a.m. Not the time-slot to set the world on fire. I hated doing that shift. Even though I knew radio was for me and I still wanted to do it, there were several reasons why I wasn't so keen on doing the Sunday overnight show. First, the music was shite. It was simulcast on both Aire FM, the pop side for the kids, and Magic 828, the AM side for the dead. The music had to be a mixture of stuff that appealed to both audiences. Bollocks. How many twenty-year-olds get their kicks from listening to Colin Blunstone's 'Say You Don't Mind'? None, is the answer, unless they had odd parents who didn't allow them to listen to 'modern-day music' and trapped them in the cellar with nothing but the Carpenters and Mason Williams (ask your parents!). Another reason I hated doing the show were the two DJs who presented the breakfast shows on Aire FM and Magic. The Magic guy was called Mark Jones. One morning he came in and asked me why I was standing up. I told him it was because it kept me alert and made me sound more awake.

'Why bother? It's the overnight show, people wanna sleep.'

People wanna sleep? During my show? Bastard. I was trying my best and this old codger was slagging me off. One morning I used a throwaway line I'd heard some old comic use. Once again, Grandad DJ was on the talkback.

'I've got that comedy album too, but I don't use any material off it.'

Fuck off, smartarse. I'm sixteen years old, for Christ's sake.

The FM DJ, Richard James, wasn't as chatty. I remember thinking that I could impress him and get him on my side if I got his records out for the first two hours, and piled them up for him to make his job a bit easier. I was also bored in the last bit of the show so it gave me something to do. He walked in the studio during the news.

'Morning, Richard, I've got your first two hours of records out for you.'

'FUCK OFF,' he replied.

Charming. I'd gone to all that trouble and he just swears at me? Well, maybe he was just tired. It happens, I suppose. The next week I decided that I wouldn't hold it against him, but I'd nevertheless cut back the enthusiasm a bit and get only his first hour of records out and piled up on the desk. In he walked.

'Morning, Richard. Hope you're feeling a bit more chatty this week!'

'OH FUCK OFF!' was his response.

Nice. I was beginning to realise why these people chose a job where they sat in a room on their own and talked to themselves. As it turned out, I've seen Richard James since and we've had a laugh about the whole 'Fuck off' business. He explained himself by saying that it was just that I was a cocky little sixteen-year-old shit and was way too jolly for six o'clock in the morning. Fair enough. No hard feelings. I think he works in Hull now. Bless him.

As I said, I suppose I am grateful to the Fish for giving me my first break, although he taught me absolutely nothing. Apart from when it comes to negotiating programme fees, when I should try to convince them I was too young to drive and claim extra taxi expenses. So you can imagine my joy when I got offered a job at the legendary Radio Luxembourg, in Luxembourg! I took *so* much pride in telling the boss that I was leaving.

'Where are you going, if you don't mind me asking?' he whimpered.

'No, not at all. Radio Luxembourg actually,' I smugly replied.

'Really? Oh wow. That's a great move for you. I always knew you'd make it.'

Oh fuck off, I thought to myself. Well, it seemed to be the correct DJ vernacular at the time.

SCHOOL IS GREAT – WHEN YOU LEAVE

7

'm not sure exactly when it was that I got bored of school, but it happened. Being brought up as a Roman Catholic by my Roman Catholic parents I ended up attending Roman Catholic schools, unsurprisingly. There aren't many differences from going to what I would call 'normal school' apart from the fact that I went to three schools. Most of my non-Catholic friends went to two. I love to be different. My first school was St Theresa's RC Primary School in Crossgates, Leeds. It's here where another difference was noticeable:

A BUNCH OF FUCKING NUNS TAUGHT ME!

How old does that make me seem? When my mum went to school in Ireland nuns taught her and she's in her bloody sixties now. But it is true, my first years of schooling and the education that went with it were taught to me by some religious women who looked like penguins. Now, I don't know what your knowledge of nuns is, so let me enlighten you. Not all nuns are nice. In fact, some of them are horrible.

Luckily for me the headmistress was a wicked nun. She was about four feet tall and was called Sister Delores. She was Irish, naturally, and had a very pleasant manner about her. Imagine a character from the *Mr Men* dressed up as a nun: 'Little Miss Nun'. That would be a good way to picture her. Now, she was nice to us kids, but not every nun there was like her. Also teaching in the school was one who, for me, was like a nun from a scary fairy story. She wore glasses, was also Irish, but was, to be quite frank, pretty horrible to me. I reckon if God could see how she used to treat me, then I bet you any money she's in for a bollocking when she gets up to the Pearly Gates.

Sister Catherine used to pick on me. When I handed in work she would give it back covered with red pen. If I left two lines empty at the bottom of the page, Sister Catherine would say I should have filled them in. If something was spelt wrong, she would circle it in red pen and reduce my mark for it. She moaned that I was always dropping my ruler and looking for attention. **I WAS EIGHT YEARS OLD, FOR GOD'S SAKE.** I got moved to the back of the class and when Mum told her if I was that much trouble then she should move me to the front, Sister Catherine replied, 'Oh he's too tall to sit at the front of the class.' Even my mum agreed that she was picking on me.

Every morning my lovely mother would send me off to school looking immaculate. Mum is a very proud person and always wanted my brother and me to look our best. We'd have clean hankies in our pockets and our dinner money would be in a special little envelope labelled 'Dinner Money'. The school asked that all pupils turn up with the exact dinner money so they didn't have to find change and it meant we all got our dinner quicker. One morning my mum was running late and didn't have the right change. School dinner must have been about 70 pence and my mum would've given me a pound. Hardly the end of the world, you'd think. Well, you'd be wrong. Sister Catherine went berserk, told me off and sent me outside to stand against the wall, the ultimate punishment for a small child who'd been given 30 pence extra in their dinner money.

The news of me being sent out of class to stand against a wall got back to my mother through the school-pupils' gossip network and she wasn't happy. She stormed up to school to see the headmistress, Sister Delores, Little Miss Nun. Mum told my headmistress that Sister Catherine obviously didn't like me and that I should be moved to another class. Go on, Mummy Moyles! The previous teacher I had at that school had once said to my mum, 'No wonder Chris is such a good boy with good marks when he comes from a family of two lovely parents.' This of course made Mum very proud, and now this nasty nun was ruining her reputation. Now, however, with my good Roman Catholic upbringing, I can look back at Sister Catherine and let her know that I forgive her. (I'm sure she's done a lot of great things over the years and is a very sweet nun!)

One of the best bits of going to primary school was when I got to sneak out of classes and attend to my altar-boy duties. Oh yes, being an altar boy was a brilliant way to bond with God, and also get out of loads of lessons. Crossgates and the surrounding areas housed a busy Catholic community and there were always funerals or baptisms that needed altar boys in their cassocks to assist the priest with his priestly duties. It was seriously lots of fun, unless you got the dreaded Father Tagney. This guy was scary. He was so tight with God that he even got promoted to Canon Tagney, which I think meant that he could call God at any time and be allowed to speak to him. During services he would stare at the congregation over his spectacles and, trust me, when he did this, even my dad pretended to be listening.

Primary school lasted five years, and after that came the wonderfully titled St Kevin's Roman Catholic Middle School. This school was for proper grown-up kids. It had stairs and about three floors. No nuns at this school, just proper teachers who moaned about the amount of marking they had to do and how little they got paid. For some reason they decided to have rugby on the PE menu. I had no interest in sport of any kind at this point in my life, let alone a sport in which big kids ran towards you as fast as they could with the sole purpose of wanting you out of their way. However, as I was a 'big lad' for my age, I got pushed into the occasional rugby lesson. This was never fun.

What was fun, though, was showing Carol Vorderman around my school. Not many people can say they did that, right? Carol did a show on Radio Aire with a feature where kids would take her round their school. I thought this was brilliant. It was a chance for me to be on the radio and say hi to all my mates. I wrote to Carol and heard nothing. Then one day, one of the other pupils told me she had heard that Carol Vorderman was turning up and I was going to be interviewed by her. **WHY DID NOBODY TELL ME?** I made my hair look cool by pouring water onto it and sat and waited for her Radio Aire car to pull into the car park. When she did turn up, I remember that she looked quite fit. (I still think she's fit actually, which is a bit weird!) I showed her round the school and she pretended to be interested. Afterwards she said that if I ever wanted to go and watch her present her show then I should write back to her. I did just as soon as I got home, and I ended up going to help her on her radio show. She even invited me to watch the TV show *Countdown* being recorded. I think she secretly thought I was cute!

Luckily middle school only lasted for four years, then I moved on to even bigger school. Mount St Mary's RC High School was my last school. By now the novelty of school had begun to wear off and I even started to get political about the whole thing. 'Why am I forced to come to school every day to work for free, and then I have to go home and do extra work for free? It's outrageous,' I would say. Nobody listened.

The only things I liked about high school were the ice-cream van that appeared at lunchtime, which was quite cool, and the control room. As the school had a huge assembly hall, it also had a separate room overlooking it where all the lights and sound were controlled. This was another great way of getting out of lessons. One year needed assistance with their assembly rehearsal; I'd be called in. The sixth-formers needed lights for their practice of their play; another lesson to be missed. It was genius. I even started up the school's first radio station. We'd broadcast to the hall when the kids were eating lunch. Every day we'd play the hits and do messages and give mentions to the other kids. Even the teachers liked it – everybody thought it was a good idea. Things were going so well that I roped in an older pupil to help me out. He was called Darren and liked his dance music. One lunchtime I left him to it so that I could go outside for a change. When I got back, many of my mates thought that Darren had gone a bit mad with his music choice.

'What the hell was that guy playing today through the speakers?' asked a mate.

'I don't know. He likes his hardcore dance, does Darren,' I replied.

'Yeah I know that, but Voodoo Rape? That's a bit strong, isn't it?'

Darren explained to me that it was called 'Voodoo Ray' and was a huge underground dance track at the time. I said that everybody thought it was 'Voodoo Rape' and we should stop playing it. Then the headmaster explained that the school radio station would be taking a break until the new term. I suppose it was my first ever firing. And it wouldn't be my last.

By the time my GCSE exams were happening, I was ready to leave school and go and explore the dizzy heights of the outside world. I'd done hospital radio, I was helping out at Radio Aire and I had a job lined up at

Radio Topshop. On our last day at school I sneaked off to a friend's house to have a Pot Noodle and a beer. He offered me some tequila. I'd never had it before and I've never had it since. I don't know what effect it was meant to have but it made me see double and brought my Pot Noodle straight back up.

I had a great time at school. I made some brilliant friends and some of them still talk to me. But I knew I needed to get out and find myself a job. Most of my friends went off to sixth form and then to university. I never wanted to do that. I spoke to my parents about the Radio Topshop job and told them that if I wanted a career in radio, instead of going to sixth-form college I could have two years' paid practice at RTS and be taken a bit more seriously. Mum reluctantly agreed and Dad said it was fine by him. So that was that, the end of my school life and, to be honest, the end of a decent education. From now on, in the real world, it would be all downhill.

Aged 16 months in my back garden.
We still have the bucket.

1976. Me aged 2 with my mum.
My fashion sense actually got WORSE after this.

For my 5th birthday I got a jumper just like my brothers. but in blue.

1983. Me and my award-winning Dad. He still looks exactly the same, I don't as I was 9 then.

1981. By looking at the body language, Can you guess which Nun liked me and which one didn't ?

Mum made me pose for this photo with Virginia, the first girl I ever fancied. I was very embarrassed.

Me and Dad after finishing a 'fun run'?!

My 12th birthday

Kieron with acne

John Kelly

Leah Carter

Me wearing a Radio 1 jacket.

Gemma Fitzimmons (another crush)

A cake

On-Air at WBHS
You didn't have to be mad to work there.
But you did to be a patient.

At Radio Aire after interviewing DJ James Whale for a school project.

nother picture of me pretending to be a DJ.   So sad.

Martine meets my Mum at my 25th in London.

The lads from Leeds United meet my Mum.

I don't know if she did though →

Ant 'n' Dec meet my Mum.

Finally getting a question right on Family Fortunes!

In Stoke wearing another fine birthday outfit.

1998, on the road. Oblivious to the fact that I've died. Ben and Dave continue working on the show.

MY FAVOURITE GUESTS

GIRLS ALOUD

Girls a-bloody-loud! Now there is a group of four gorgeous women!

Look, let me clear this up. Sarah is quite obviously fit. So is Cheryl Tweedy. Kimberly is very pretty and she's from Bradford so I have a bit of a soft spot for her. Nadine I have met the fewest times, but again is a fine-looking woman. And then there's Nicola. Now it's fair to say that I have given Nicola a bit of ribbing on air. I have made comments for a cheap laugh, but that's what I do. They're only jokes and I hope that she can just brush them off as silly DJ remarks. But let's be fair now. In the beginning, she was known as:

THE ROPEY-LOOKING GINGER ONE AT THE BACK.

Come on. You know that's what you thought. Remember the 'Sound of The Underground' song, their first single? Have you ever seen the video? She's at the back. Hidden away behind a barbed-wire fence. You only get to see her about three times during the whole song. I don't know why it was, but maybe it was because she didn't look as ... how can I put it ... showbiz, perhaps, as the others. The other four girls were bright, sassy, sexy and in your face. Nicola was ... well, she was sour-pussed and ginger. I don't want to be horrible but I need to revisit this to explain why I sometimes take the piss out of her a bit.

You know, let me just take a break for one moment and explain how hard it is to be me sometimes. As I sit here and tap away on my keyboard, I have no plan about what I'm going to say. I just type and it appears on the screen. It's the same as the radio show. I open my mouth and I say stuff. I have millions, not thousands, but *millions* of people listening to the show waiting for me to make them smile. If I'm lucky, laugh their arse off. To do this, I have to say a range of things from exactly what you're thinking right now, to the last thing you'd expect me to say.

THIS IS WHAT I DO.

I'm not a bad person. I genuinely don't want to upset anybody. Well, there are a few I wouldn't mind upsetting. But generally speaking I don't. Look, most of my audience know that I'm a nice guy. Off air, I'm quiet, shy almost. On air I come alive. It's just the way I am. So sometimes I say things for a cheap laugh. You know the kind of comments you make down the pub or in college or in the office with your mates. It's a joke. They're just words.

Right, where was I? Oh yeah, the ginger one. Look, in this job I meet a lot of famous people. Pop stars have come and gone. In my time at Radio 1 I have already outlived many bands. 5ive. 911. Bewitched. A1. S Club 7. Blue. Remember any of them? All of them have done well. Then finished.

During their 'time at the top', their 'moment of greatness', members of these bands get tired. It's understandable. They work long hours and, contrary to popular belief, are not on that much money. Not at the start anyway. Early starts, lots of interviews, travelling miles and miles in the one car 'cos it's cheaper. It's hard. Sometimes Mr or Mrs Popstar gets tired. Their fake smile drops and they can get a bit moody. Bring on Nicola from Girls Aloud. The first time I met her she had a face like a slapped arse. Seriously. She just looked like she wanted to go home. Even on TV she can look like she's been pushed on stage against her will. I know it's hard but:

IT'S YOUR FUCKING JOB!

And because they have all had their media training, they don't feel comfortable telling a slightly fat DJ such as myself: 'Look, do me a favour, man. I've been on the go all week. I'm tried and it's radio. I ain't smiling!'

That would do. I would be cool with that. But it doesn't happen. I'm an OK guy; I get how the pop star thing works. Look, Cheryl was happy coming into the studio one morning without a stitch of make-up on. She's a pretty girl but I gotta say the make-up helps. I had a laugh with her and she was cool about it. Nicola would just glare at me or look away with an expression on her face that reads:

'THIS GUY IS A COCK.'

Maybe I am a cock. She's done nothing to me so why should I have a go at her? It's a fair comment. Which is why I explained earlier that I don't mean it. I'm just having some fun. She has recently been a bit better with me and so I'm trying to build a bridge of friendship between us. Also 'cos I hope to get off with one of the others and it might help. So, just to recap, the reasons I take the mickey out of Nicola are:

GINGER
MOODY FACE
THINKS I'M A COCK

Cheryl, as I said, is different. I like her. I think she's funny. Kimberly is very friendly and seems like a really top girl. Nadine was always ill when I met the others so I've only really met her a few times but, again, seems ace. Plus she's Irish, which is always a winner with me. Then there's Sarah. Do I even need to say anything about how gorgeous she is? She makes me wish I were better-looking.

Now I must point out that I don't know them *that* well. They're certainly not friends (although how cool to be proper friends with people who are beautiful, sexy and talented for a living). If the girls walked into Radio 1 one day and saw me, I know at least three of them would say hello to me. Maybe four. I'd love it if it were all five. Seriously, I'd love to be friends with Girls Aloud. Just imagine how great that would be. Kimberly calling me up to see if I'm back home for Christmas and did I want to meet for a drink. Cheryl asking me if I was going to the next England friendly and did I need a lift. Sarah calling me up to cry on my shoulder 'cos another hunk has let her down.

WHAT A LOSER I AM.

Why do these girls have this effect on me? Last time I saw them, Sarah smiled at me. They were doing an interview for TV somewhere and I started jumping about trying to make them laugh. Jesus Christ, I was like a fucking child. It was so embarrassing. Just 'cos some pretty girls have waved at me I'm acting like a right twat. What do I think will happen? If I act like a dick, then Sarah will think I'm cute and want to go out with me? Oh my God. Maybe Nicola is right.

MAYBE I AM A COCK!

Well, anyway, Girls Aloud are ace. And Nicola, just in case you are reading this, I wish you all the luck in the world. I genuinely hope that you have a successful life, make a lot of money and are very happy. Just do me a favour and:

GIVE US A FUCKING SMILE FROM TIME TO TIME!

Thank you.

9

3

After eighteen months as a DJ on Radio Aire, I had started looking to move on to bigger and better things. I made demo tapes and sent them out to bosses at other radio stations in the hope that they would listen to the tape, be impressed, then call me and offer me a job. The truth, though, was that you would send a tape to a station, hear nothing, call the person you'd sent the tape to and either not get through to them *ever*, or get through to them only to be told there isn't anything going at the moment. Before I got the job at Radio 1, I worked for several different stations and sending out demo tapes became second nature to me, the sending-out-of-demo-tapes task was a military procedure that went like this:

Buy blank cassette tapes.

Buy Jiffy bags and blank address labels for Jiffy bags.

**Get station cassette labels and
write your name and number on them.**

This was very important. You had to write your name and phone number on the cassette box and the cassette itself, in case they misplaced the box, wanted to call you, but couldn't find your number. Apparently radio station bosses were stupid.

Go through *lots* of tapes and edit together your best bits.

This was a laborious task that always ended up with me editing late into the night in a small studio at the radio station.

Dub the best bits onto the cassette tapes labelled with your name and, of course, your all-important phone number.

Dubbing tapes was like water torture. After spending days picking out the best bits, you then had to listen to them again and again as you copied the cassettes.

**Write a letter to the boss of the station explaining
why they should hire you.**

I still maintain that if you put '**I am cheap**' in bold at the top of the letter, it
will usually get read.

**Create a CV that makes you look better than you are.
Include *anything* remotely impressive.**

I always put on the bottom of my CV, 'Numerous referees available on
request', as I didn't actually have any references.

Check the letter, the CV, the tapes and the labels.

Package up, and send off.

Keep a note of the people you sent your tapes to.

This was so I could call them to check they got the tape. More often than not I never got through, but at least I could make phone pals with the receptionist, who would get to know me because I would be calling with no success every week for about six weeks.

Occasionally, I got a job from doing this. One time at Radio Aire I sent out nine demo tapes. I thought I'd better send out one more, just to round the number up to ten. Tony Adams, he of the complicated features, had recently left Radio Aire to work at Radio Luxembourg, so I thought I might as well send one there. I knew I wouldn't get a job, but I might get a nice letter or something. I was wrong. I didn't get a letter. I got a job instead. It was a week before my eighteenth birthday. Jeff Graham was the boss. A Scottish guy with wild curly hair who seemed quite stern on the phone, but was nice enough. I later found out he was indeed nice, albeit with a fiery temper.

Before I go on I need to answer a question that has been asked of me ever since I took the job, back in 1992.

Yes. Radio Luxembourg was based in Luxembourg.

It amazed me, the amount of people who thought it was just some catchy name, or that it broadcast from a ship in the middle of the sea. No, it didn't. It was broadcast from new state-of-the-art studios just outside Luxembourg's city centre.

When Jeff Graham called me, he was initially interested but wanted to hear more. Instead of an edited tape, he wanted me to record my next show and send it to him. I had already started to work out how I could edit it to make it sound better yet still give the impression that it was a 'live' tape, when he called back a few days later.

'Don't worry about the other tape. You've got the job.'

I was eighteen years old and about to head out to Luxembourg to work for one of the most famous radio stations ever. I didn't even know where the hell Luxembourg was. I thought at one point it was near Pakistan. Then somebody else thought it was in a desert. It's actually kind of in the middle of Europe between France and Germany and somewhere else. OK, I'm still not 100 per cent sure. I went by plane for Christ's sake. I didn't drive. Even though I didn't know where it was, I didn't care. It was a move in the right direction, far better than I could have imagined. Oh, and they paid more than £39 a show too! One of the reasons Jeff offered me the job was after a phone call he had with another DJ, Mark Page. Mark had previously worked for Radio 1 and was now hosting the breakfast show at Radio Aire. I didn't know him that well but our paths had crossed often enough and I was a huge fan of his. Jeff told Mark he had asked me for another tape. Mark convinced Jeff that he didn't need another tape and should hire me immediately. There are many people that I need to thank for helping me along the way, and Mark Page is one of them. Thank you, Mark. Despite the fact that I had to work with Jeff Graham for a year, I'm very grateful for your help.

About two weeks after my eighteenth birthday, I headed out to Luxy. When I arrived, I was immediately met with my first problem.

I had to change my name!

It turned out that Jeff had hired two new DJs. A scrawny-looking camp fella by the name of Jonathan Miles, and me, Chris Moyles. Jeff thought the two surnames, Miles and Moyles, were too similar, and because I had the least experience, I should change my name. I came up with many possible alternatives:

Chris Mass

Chris Packet

Chris 't' Lord (not my mother's favourite)

Chris Pandry

Chris Peacock

I wanted to keep it as close to my own name as possible. Changing it to Mike somebody or Simon somebody would just feel like I was lying to the audience about who I was. (What a dick! It turned out we only had about twelve listeners anyway, and there was me thinking about my huge loyal audience.) In the end I chose Chris Holmes. Holmes was my mother's maiden name so I thought it was a nice touch. Plus it didn't sound too DJ-like. I was the fill-in DJ on the station, but as the DJs had six weeks' holiday each, I was pretty much always working. I started in March 1992. I had hit the big time.

The first thing they did when Jonathan and I arrived was to put us up for two weeks in a hotel in a place called Limpertsberg … or something like that. We were introduced to the other DJs and staff and went out for dinner the first night for one of the ex-DJs' birthdays. The whole team seemed really nice. A few of them, it has to be said, were a bit quirky. In no particular order there was:

Jeff Graham: programme director, who was very friendly but had *the* worst temper on a man I had ever seen.

John Catlett: station manager. An American man who seemed to serve no purpose whatsoever other than to tell us off for calling home so much on the studio telephones. He was short and in his fifties and had an obsession with paper clips. If anybody in the office ever said they needed one, John's soft American accent would be heard saying, 'Paper clips? I have some.' Odd.

Jodie Scott: a small, chubby Canadian DJ who had been there for so long

I genuinely think she'd gone native. She was very sweet, though, and really nice to me. She also played guitar and sang.

Wendy Lloyd: a young, tall, gorgeous girl who was very eager and wasn't afraid to tell you that you were wrong and she was right. We became good pals during our time there and still keep in touch. She never held back on saying what she wanted to say. I drunkenly snogged her on the night of my twenty-fifth birthday and she critiqued me on it afterwards. That was Wendy.

Jonathan Miles: the other new boy at the station. What Jonathan didn't teach me about being camp and bitchy isn't worth knowing. The nicest drama queen I have ever met.

Tony Adams: the DJ from Radio Aire in Leeds. He again was working the night shift. Now this man was odd. He rented a house *miles* away from the radio station. On his first night there, he realised that the road outside was too noisy to allow him to sleep, so he was forced to sleep in his bathroom at the back of the house. I swear it's true.

Mike Hollis: Mike was in his forties and from Birmingham. He had previously managed the comedian Lenny Henry and had been at Luxembourg for years. He was a proper legend, a family man, and a guy who didn't take things too seriously. He also loved a beer. Unsurprisingly, we became good pals.

So there I was. Eighteen years old, and these were to be my new friends in a new country. A hyperactive young sexy woman. A camp gay guy with money problems. An American guy who loved paper clips. A boss whose temper flared up quicker than a guy with a nut allergy after eating Revels, and a Canadian woman who had lived in Luxembourg for so long that her idea of a great night out was a trip to a bar called the French Café. I know

French people who wouldn't hang out in a bar full of French people. And Tony Adams, the guy who slept in his bathroom. The station only had five of us DJs, together with the two bosses and an office secretary. The studios and offices were based in a big media building run by the owners RTL. Inside were floors of other studios and radio stations. French, German and local Luxembourg people all worked there. And then us, the weird little English family. Because there were only a few of us, we hung out together. Wendy, Jonathan and Mike were probably my main buddies, but I got on well with everybody

Mike Hollis was like my brother, dad and friendly uncle all rolled into one man. During that first night out, a few of us ended up drinking until the early hours. When I went into the office the next day saying a cheery 'Good morning,' I was met with hungover faces and groans from the rest of the staff. I had just turned eighteen so drinking lots of lager was what I did. I felt fine and raring to go. The rest of the staff looked like they'd just sat through an evening of Anthea Turner's holiday photos. With Anthea Turner. Mike Hollis came over to me.

'Hey, that was a good drink last night. You feeling OK after it?'

'Yeah,' I said. 'I feel great.'

He looked at me and gave me a huge smile. 'I think I've just found my new drinking buddy,' he said.

And he wasn't lying. Mike introduced me to Bitburger lager. It's German, and strong. The rest of the stories about me and Mike drinking are a blur.

Another day, Wendy and I were doing our laundry at a place in town. I was meant to be recording some overnight music shows but I had my mum and dad coming over to see me so I wanted to get some clothes clean. I must point out at this part of the story that not only had I never done laundry before, on account of having lived with my parents all my life, I had also never done laundry in Luxembourg before. My machine filled up with water, and stayed like that for about an hour. This was a problem. I was meant to be at work recording these two-hour music shows, but I had a machine full of soaking-wet Simpsons boxer shorts and C&A socks. I was getting panicky and Wendy was getting angry with me.

'Call Jeff and tell him you'll be late 'cos your machine broke down. It's simple.'

Well, that seemed to make sense. I couldn't just turn up at work with a huge bag full of dripping pants, could I?

WRONG!

As I've mentioned, my boss, Jeff Graham had an amazing temper. He was a nice man, but when his buttons were pressed, and sometimes when they weren't, he would yell. Loudly. Regardless of who you were. So what the hell would he be like with a snotty eighteen-year-old DJ from Leeds? So yeah, I was a bit worried about calling him to tell him I was going to be an hour late for work. But Wendy had convinced me that it would be fine.

WRONG AGAIN!

Jeff went ballistic. He started shouting at me, telling me he didn't care where I was and I had better get my arse into work or else. He screamed at me so loudly down the phone that Wendy could hear him over the other washing machines and dryers. She could see it was a silly argument so she took the phone out of my hand and tried to explain to Jeff that I was going to be late and it wasn't really a big problem. Thirty seconds later, after Jeff had started shouting at her, she began shouting and swearing back.

'Oh just shut the fuck up and calm down.'

As far as I was aware Wendy had had no previous NATO experience but seemed to be handling the situation … erm … badly, actually. I did thank her for trying, though – about fifteen minutes later, in her car, with a bag of dripping wet underpants on my lap.

There are other stories I could tell you about my time in Luxembourg, but they'd fill up a book of their own. Don't even get me started on my gay friend Jonathan's stories of masturbating and the fact that he walked round his flat naked all the time smoking a cigarette like some character out of *Dynasty*. But they were a great bunch of people and I had the best time ever there.

I later found out that they all had bets on how long I would last before I threw a wobbler and left. Some had me down for three months. The worst was about six weeks. However, I proved them all wrong and stayed until the end. It was no big effort really. The station closed down nine months after I arrived!

One day John Catlett, the big boss, gathered us all together and told us the sad news. They were going to close down Radio Luxembourg for ever. As much as this was shocking to hear, it was hardly a massive surprise. The station's transmitters, so we were told, cost hundreds of thousands of pounds to maintain. The radio station was making no money. And I mean no money. Our only income came from a paid-for religious radio show that lasted fifteen minutes and was called 'Radio Outreach'. I knew this was true because I had to sit there once a week at the weekend and play the tape in. A guy would sit in his studio at home and read stuff from the

Bible and play hymns for quarter of an hour every week. When the show finished, I'd play a big Radio Luxembourg jingle and then kick off the *Saturday Night Dance Party*.

'Thanks be to God for the last fifteen minutes. Here's Betty Boo with "Doing The Doo"!'

We were told that our last night was to be 30 December 1992. After that, we were all jobless. Everybody in the office went silent for about thirty seconds. Until I asked:

'Does that mean we can use the phones in the studio to call home again then?'

My dad and my brother Kieron came out to Luxembourg for a visit just after Christmas. They were going to hang out with me for a few days as I said goodbye to what had been my home for ten months. By now I had found places to eat and drink and was becoming quite the local so it was really cool to show them around this amazing, if slightly quiet, place. On their first night, we grabbed some food and then headed to a bar for a few drinks, the Moyles men together, drinking foreign lager in a bar in Luxembourg. It was nice, just the three of us having a few drinks as I bored them silly with my stories. Being eighteen and living in Luxembourg for almost a year had shown me lots of things I wasn't used to back home. Don't get me wrong; it wasn't like going back in time to another world or anything. It wasn't actually *that* different, but certain things were better. One of the first things I noticed, and absolutely loved, was the fact that:

McDONALD'S SOLD BEER!

Seriously, how great was that? You could have a Big Mac and a lager for your lunch. For me, this was heaven itself. Although I did spend way too much time there.

Another thing was the fact that when you ordered fries anywhere:

THEY GAVE YOU A LITTLE TUB OF MAYONNAISE!

Now this may seem normal to you, the modern-day book-reader of the twenty-first century, but trust me, back then, to an eighteen-year-old from Leeds, this was wicked. I quickly became addicted to chips and mayo. There, I said it. I was an addict.

At Christmas in the town square, where the aforementioned burger/beer place was, they would put on a market selling all sorts of Christmas presents. I was used to markets, Leeds having the biggest indoor market in Europe, but it wasn't anything like that. There wasn't that familiar stench of fresh vegetables and fish like there was back home. This market had incense-burning Father Christmas ornaments. It sold cute little carved wooden nativity scenes, and all manner of gorgeous yet completely useless crap that your mother would love as a gift. (The pipe-smoking Santa still makes an appearance on the mantelpiece in Mum and Dad's living room every Christmas.) The shops were a godsend to somebody like me at Christmas. The staff were always very helpful. They could also tell immediately that English was by far my strongest language and would therefore speak to me in a tongue I understood. But the best bit about shopping in Luxembourg at Christmas was that when you were buying something at the till, they would ask you if it was a present for somebody, and if it was:

THEY WOULD WRAP IT FOR YOU!

What a simple stroke of genius. You buy a framed picture of Mickey Mouse (Jonathan really loved Mickey Mouse) and they would wrap it for you.

By the time you got home, you're all done. None of that sitting on your knees on the floor with bits of sellotape stuck to your nose while you waste far too much paper wrapping it badly. No, sir. For the locals in Luxembourg, it's done before you even leave the shop. Another example of what great ideas they had. Or maybe it was proof that the place was full of lazy, alcoholic mayonnaise addicts.

Anyway, so there we were. My dad, my brother and me, sitting in a bar drinking lager on my last night in Luxembourg. After a few beers, my dad decided to call it a night. He did, after all, have to drive us all the way back to Leeds, which was a hell of a journey. Kieron and I decided to walk into town and find a few more bars.

Now as I said, when we landed in Luxy, the radio station put us up for two weeks in a hotel. After that you were on your own. Luckily I found a nice studio flat with a tiny kitchen, tiny bathroom and a tiny living room with a cove in the corner that housed my bed. It wasn't big at all, but it was mine, and I thought it was cool as fuck. It even had a tiny balcony that overlooked the dirty-looking street outside. I was so European. As far as I remember the estate agents that found me the flat charged one month's rent in advance, one month's rent commission for finding the place and one month's rent deposit. This turned out to be a hell of a lot of money. Luckily, with a little advance from work, I got the money together and waited patiently at *les estate agents* for the landlord to turn up so I could get the keys. After a while, a cool-looking blue sports car pulled up. I'm not into cars, but it looked the mutt's nuts. Small and sleek, with a sports-car engine roar that makes your head turn. This landlord must be one flash bastard, I thought to myself. Once again, I was wrong. The door swung open to reveal a frail old man who looked about eighty-five – I swear on my life. He looked like a pale version of Yoda from *Star Wars*.

And he had a walking stick. Worse than that, he was obviously very very rich, what with at least one extra home and a really, really cool-looking sports car.

WHAT A LUCKY OLD BASTARD!

I reminisced about this and my stories of mayonnaise and Christmas presents that wrap themselves as my brother and I downed a few more beers late into the night. Eventually, after I realised that my speech had gone from a slur to that of its own language only understood by me, we decided it was time to wander back to the flat. I remember getting inside, having one more beer from the fridge, then settling down on the mattress on the floor to a good drunken night's sleep.

'Morning, drunkard,' said my dad. 'Where's your brother?'

These were not the words I needed to hear on my final morning in Luxembourg.

'I don't know. Is he in the loo?' I replied.

'Nope,' said Dad, as he and I both took on the same facial expression. The kind of face that looks confused and worried but more importantly says:

WHERE THE FUCK IS MY DICKHEAD BROTHER?

Back then we didn't have mobile phones. Back in early 1993 mobile phones were for rich people or yuppie-looking dickheads. We had no way of contacting him or indeed finding out where the hell he could have been.

'By the way, what is this?' asked my dad, holding up half a snapped-off towel rail from the bathroom.

'Bloody hell, what has he done!'

I was moving out and back to England in about an hour and a half. Just after the rich sports-car-driving almost-dead landlord had checked on the flat, so I could get my deposit back. A deposit that was about £500 and which I needed, because I had no job. After an hour, we finally spotted my brother stumbling down the street.

'Where the hell have you been?' I screamed from my tiny balcony.

'Hey, man. I went looking for some glue,' he slurred.

Turns out that after I went to sleep, he decided to go for a pee. Drunk and wobbly, he lost his balance and grabbed the towel rail for support. It didn't work, surprise sur-fucking-prise, and snapped off. With brains that only a drunken older brother would have, he decided to walk into a town he didn't know, looking for a twenty-four-hour garage that didn't exist, trying to find some glue to buy with the money he didn't have, to fix the towel rail with the towel-rail-fixing experience he didn't possess. Surprisingly, he didn't succeed. He did, however, find a bar, continue drinking and wobble back to the flat drunk. And this is my older brother that I look up to!

Anyway, we decided to leave the broken towel rail and some money, and we set off for home. My proper home, in Leeds, where I would once again live with Mum and Dad. And my genius brother.

MY FAVOURITE GUESTS

DALE WINTON

Dale is a brilliant radio guest. I'd have him on air with us any time he wanted. He gets what we do, which is always a bonus – and is maybe because he was a radio broadcaster before he broke into television – and he just makes the show light up. He is perfect for a show like ours: he laughs a lot, his camp humour is great, and I love the way he uses the fact that he's openly gay to play around and have fun, usually at our expense. He plays the gay card well but equally very subtly sometimes, like when Dave mentioned his wife one day on the air. Dale immediately asked Dave:

'Oh, are you married?'

'Yes, I am, Dale.'

'Oh. What a waste.'

One Saturday morning he greeted me on air with a line about my recently shaved-off goatee beard.

'Oh I did love your beard, Moylesy, but I did worry it would leave a rash on my inner thigh.'

Beautiful image, I'm sure you'll agree. Dale plays the camp bitch to a tee. I love camp humour so the two of us work very well together. He also knows his stuff about the business and is *very* professional. Every time he's on the show we'll nip off for a fag break (no pun intended) and he'll ask how things are going and we'll talk about radio and television. I'm sure he still does want to turn me into a fully fledged gay though.

ELTON JOHN

Elton came on the show in late 2004 wanting to play a brand new track he was involved with. Now, normally with acts such as Elton, there are rules about playing their new track. Sadly, when it comes to the 'more established artists' (a polite way of saying older ones), many people consider their new material to be rubbish. This is before they have even heard it. It's a general rule of thumb that sweeps through Radio 1. The simple equation would be this:

OLDER ARTIST = CRAP NEW MATERIAL

Sometimes, though, a guest is offered to you who may be too good to turn down. Paul McCartney is another good example of this. The guy is amazing, has written some of the greatest British music ever, yet who wants to hear his new stuff? Not many people, is the answer. It's not that it's rubbish, although most of the time it is, it's just that it's not usually suited to the

Radio 1 audience. Therefore there are rules in place to prevent rubbish new music being played on the air by legendary artists. I don't necessarily agree with these rules, but here they are anyway.

RULES FOR PLAYING OLDER ARTISTS' NEW TRACKS ON AIR

Don't.

Try anything you can not to play it. It will be rubbish.

If you have to, play a short clip of it, then move on.

If they insist on all of it, talk over the last minute of it to save the listeners from boredom.

Harsh but fair, I think. So Elton John is booked to come on the show. I am very excited. I really like him, both as a performer and as a personality. (He'll probably hate me for calling him a personality now!) I'd been trying to get him on the show for years, thinking that our humour would suit him perfectly. By coincidence, he was booked to come on the show the same day as ex-No Doubt lead singer and now solo performer Gwen Stefani. When 'stars' turn up to our show we like to guess how many people they will bring with them. Gwen did not disappoint: her entourage consisted of four silly dancers, a minder, various record company people, and I'm sure there was a make-up artist too. As we were finishing the interview with Gwen, Elton turned up. He had with him his manager, and his record company person, and that was it. Gwen had about ten people accompany her to the studio; Elton John had two. I loved that. With all guests we walk them into the studio 'live'. I do this because it means that there are no uncomfortable silences before they speak on air, and so that the audience hears their first reaction. I also think it's quite cool, as nobody else does this. Elton gets walked into our studio and immediately things take an interesting turn.

'Good morning, Elton John.'

'Good morning, Chris Moyles,' says Elton.

'Is this early for you, Elton?'

'Yeah, it is. It shows you how long it is since I've been to Radio 1. We went to the wrong building and ended up at Broadcasting House. I saw Tony Blackburn walking down the corridor and thought to myself: hang on a second, I think we've got the wrong fucking place here.'

WHOOPS!

'Elton, you can't swear on the air, take that back, please.' I was loving it already.

'We're not on the air now, are we?' He genuinely looked shocked.

'Yes, we are. So apologies for the f-word and no more swearing, please, Elton.'

Swearing is such a problem at Radio 1 you would not believe it. I knew Elton would be lively and I have no problems with that, but if a guest does swear, I have to apologise immediately and tell them not to swear again. We can get fined for guests swearing.

ANYWAY, BACK TO MY STORY!

Once Elton had sworn on the air, he was like a child being told not to say the word 'why'. We played his new track, 'Ghetto Gospel', which ended up being brilliant. A mix of a Tupac track with an old Elton song that was absolutely suited to our audience. It just goes to show, I suppose. Once Elton was in the swing of things, he got really relaxed and swore again. It was fairly mild and I thought it was funny. Then it got worse. It was funny radio and I knew that my audience would love it, but at the same time I gotta watch my back and try to keep the swearing to a minimum.

'You can't say tits on the radio, can you?' said Elton, referring to a Scissor Sisters track of the same name.

'No, you can't say that, Elton, no,' I replied.

'Can I say wank?'

That was Elton John, ladies and gentlemen. His eyes lit up as he was saying it. I knew that we would get complaints but I also thought that it was funny, so what can you do? We got the usual press in the national red tops and things went on as normal. I saw Elton a few weeks later at BBC Television Centre for *Children in Need* night. When he saw me he asked if I had got into trouble for him swearing on air.

'No, it was fine.'

'Are you sure? I wouldn't want you getting into shit for something I had said.'

'No, honestly, it was fine. But thanks anyway.'

'Well fuck 'em. I didn't say anything that bad anyway.'

Incidentally, 'Ghetto Gospel' went straight to number one.

I LOVE ELTON JOHN.

9

BACK HOME AND OUT OF WORK

1

I returned from Luxembourg with my entire studio flat of belongings rammed into my dad's Astra. We drove from Luxembourg all the way back to Leeds. The car was so full that the guys at passport control were confused when we handed them three passports instead of two. Then they saw Kieron's hand waving at them from behind a rolled-up duvet and two large boxes. It was a long, cramped journey, but it got me home in one piece.

It's a weird feeling when you don't have a job. Weird in many ways, especially as I hadn't been fired or left of my own free will. The radio station closed down so I didn't have a job. I wasn't particularly worried, not at first anyway, but as I believed that my job at Radio Luxembourg had come about more by luck than anything else I had no idea how easy or difficult it would be to find another one. My dad has always disagreed with me when I've said I've been lucky, but I think I have been.

'You're not lucky. You've worked hard to get where you are,' he'd say.

Now don't get me wrong, I *have* worked hard. In fact, I've worked my bollocks off. I worked hard to get my jobs and then worked harder still to keep them. Now, at Radio 1, it's even more important that I stay fresh and consistent. When you present the flagship show for BBC Radio 1, *everybody* wants your job. I don't care what certain other DJs say, they would give their left testicle to do this gig. Trust me, this is my business, I know, and I also know who they are. The smug DJ on lots of money on the London station, he wants my job. The guy on Virgin Radio, who says he's not interested, he is desperate for my job. Virtually every single breakfast-show presenter on local radio in the UK, they all want my job. Well, if you're reading this, here's the news.

YOU AIN'T GONNA GET IT.

Hard as I have worked, I have been equally lucky. If I hadn't been fired from a radio station in Bradford, I would never have been desperate enough to take the job in Stoke. If it wasn't for meeting a record-plugger in Stoke who liked the show, he would never have mentioned me to the boss of Chiltern Radio. If the boss there wasn't pals with the boss at Capital Radio, I would never have got that job. And if I hadn't worked at Capital, I wouldn't have got the job at Radio 1, and wouldn't have written this book. That means you would be sitting wherever you're sitting with your hands out on front of you holding nothing and looking like a mental person.

I left Luxembourg with a contract pay-off of about £6,000, which I thought would come in handy for a rainy day when I couldn't find a new job. I wasn't to know then that it would piss it down for a few weeks.

I was speaking to a guy called Steve Martin – not the American comedian and actor, before you start – a radio boss who was running a station in Bradford called the Pulse. He liked my tape but told me there wasn't anything going yet and he wasn't in a position to hire me at that point. I was to keep in touch and let him know of any developments. I then spoke to a guy who was starting up a brand new radio station in Carlisle. He chatted to me on the phone and seemed extremely enthusiastic about my plans and ideas, so I drove up to Carlisle to meet him and see the studios. I called Steve Martin and explained that I would probably have to make my decision there and then. He told me I should take the job, as he still wasn't ready to offer me anything.

I got to Carlisle to see the studios, but there weren't any. The radio station, still being built, was currently in two Portakabins in the car park of Border Television. Not exactly what I was used to from Luxembourg, but the guy seemed nice enough and I decided to take the job presenting the evening show. I was to move to Carlisle and join the station for the launch. Pay packet: £14,000. I drove back to Leeds and went to bed.

First thing the next morning, the phone rang. It was Steve Martin from the radio station down the road in Bradford.

'I'm now in a position to offer you a job,' he told me.

YOU ARE HAVING A FUCKING LAUGH?

'On your advice I've just told this guy that I'd take his job in Carlisle,' I screamed back.

'Well, don't take it. Can you come in and see me straight away in my office?'

I did. He offered me the evening show on the Pulse. The job was for £15,000. Not only one thousand pounds more money, but also it was in Bradford, which meant I could live at home with Mum and Dad and not have to move to Carlisle. I accepted the job then went home all excited, if not a little pissed off for having to mess people around. I called the guy in Carlisle; he was not a happy man.

'What do you mean, you've changed your mind? You accepted the job and you gave me your word that you were going to take it,' he yelled.

'Yeah, well, I am really sorry about that, but I've been offered the same show for more money and it's local to me so I wouldn't have to move, meaning that I save more money still,' I calmly explained.

'Oh really? So if I offered you even more money than that, you'd turn him down and come and work with us in Carlisle, would you?'

Now this was a weird situation. Here I was, just turned nineteen years old and out of work. A grown man and a radio station boss was asking me whether, if he paid me more money to do the same show, I would change my mind again and come and work for him. It didn't take too long for me to answer him.

'Of course I would,' I said.

'I see. That's how your loyalties lie, do they?'

WHAT WAS HE TALKING ABOUT?

I may have been a young kid, but I'm not going to be treated like an idiot. He needed telling.

'Listen, with all due respect, if you offered me more money to come and work for you, of course I'd say yes. I love radio, don't get me wrong, but this is my business. If I'm to move all the way to Carlisle it has to be worth my while. So yes, I would take it.'

He didn't let up. 'Well, I think that's the wrong attitude to have,' he replied, smugly.

OH PISS OFF.

This guy was beginning to get on my tits. It's the same time slot on a different radio station. What the hell am I meant to answer with? *Actually, you're right. I'm a man of morals and a man of my word. And even though I haven't signed a contract with you, I will turn down more money to work on a radio station twenty minutes' away to work for less money two hundred miles away, for, by the way, a radio station …*

THAT DOESN'T EVEN HAVE ANY FUCKING STUDIOS BUILT YET!

Anyway, I apologised again and said that if he needed any help getting the station off the ground then he shouldn't hesitate to call me. I admit, looking back, that this might have seemed like a sarcastic gesture, but it really wasn't, I promise. I have worked out some of this business, but not all of it.

He declined my polite offer and told me I would never get anywhere with this kind of attitude towards work. Really? Well, fuck you, mister £14,000-a-year-in-a-Portakabin-in-a-fucking-car-park man. I am not a child. I am an adult who makes adult decisions. So I'm staying at home with my mummy and my daddy, and balls to you.

The Pulse was originally called Pennine Radio. Then it changed its name to the Pulse or Pulse FM. It was quite confusing, which one it was actually called, so the first thing the new boss did was to change it to the Pulse. Nice and simple. Its studios were in the basement of a building on Forster Square right next to Bradford city centre. The studios were a bit crappy and all the DJs had to share a room with the news department, but it was my new home nonetheless.

There were some decent DJs there. Not all of them decent, but some of them. Elliott Webb had just been moved to the Big Breakfast show with his co-host Debbie Lindley, who had large breasts and was a very nice girl. Now you may think that the size of her breasts is inconsequential and sexist, but trust me, they were huge. A guy called Alex Rowlands presented the lunchtime show. He was kind of suave and sophisticated and did a feature creatively entitled 'Eat to the Beat'. Genius. The afternoon guy was Andy Brown. He was replaced shortly after I arrived. I don't remember if he knew he was about to be replaced, but on his last show he took a request from an old woman who wanted to hear some Joe Longthorne. Sadly, the only record he could find of Joe's was a Christmas album. So he played a Christmas track – in the middle of April. A young man called James Cridland, who went by the DJ name of James Andrews, replaced Andy. James would later prove himself to be my only real friend at the station.

The first time I was introduced to James was by a woman at the station called Jayne Young. She was American, or something, and was like the boss's number two. She also had a voice that reminded you of dragging your fingernails down a blackboard. She wasn't very tactful either.

'This is James,' she said, introducing me to the newest member of the team. 'He's going to be doing the afternoon show. Now, he has a stutter, but you can't tell when he's on air.'

Charming. What an introduction that was. James looked sheepishly at me and said hi. Oddly, the Yank turned out to be telling the truth. James did have an ever so slight stutter, but when he was on air it *never* came out. Bless him. James was also further evidence that DJs are the untidiest people on the planet. He always had an unironed shirt and looked a bit scruffy. One day he gave me a lift in his car. At my feet in the passenger side were several empty burger boxes and sandwich wrappers. His whole car was like a bin.

I liked James straight away. We got on well and shared the same twisted sense of humour. One day we spent a few hours in the studio doing a mickey-take recording of the entire radio station. We called it the Piss and did impressions of all the other DJs on the station, highlighting any odd habit they had and having a laugh with it. It wasn't difficult to do – the place was full of potential. The news editor was a naturist who enjoyed being naked with other naturists. One of his news reporters sounded like he was talking with a peg on his nose. The breakfast girl had big boobs and the commercial production people who made the adverts were all insane. Add to that the fact that the radio station played the same records over and over again. So on our tape we put Go West's 'Call Me', an 1980s classic, on repeat.

This tape has been circulating ever since. If you want a copy, speak to our friend Simon Hirst: he's got lots of embarrassing tapes of mine!

Boss Steve Martin was a fairly quiet man who had been sent down from the group's HQ in Newcastle to sort out this radio station, which was underachieving. From the start I got the impression he wasn't massively happy moving to Bradford. I got that impression from him when he told me:

'They've sent me here to fix this place. And that's what I'm going to do. And when I've done that, I'm getting straight out of here and going back to Newcastle.'

What a lovely welcome. He made me feel like this was the best place in the world to work.

I got to work presenting the evening show by immediately changing the name of the programme to 'The Chris Moyles Evening Bit'. Clever, eh? I started phoning round the record companies for guests and competition prizes. Suddenly some of the music industry's biggest names were on my show. Kenny Thomas. Lindy Layton. Kim Appleby. Shara Nelson. Oh yeah. I was mixing with the big stars. I also called up the local cinema and asked if they did press screenings. They did and were only too happy to invite me to see all the new films for free. What a job this was turning out to be. Everything was going well until one afternoon I got called into the boss's office.

Now, Steve spoke v-e-r-y s-l-o-w-l-y i-n-d-e-e-d.

'You know, Chris, for this radio station to succeed, everybody needs to play their part, and I've noticed that you don't really have a part.'

I had no idea what he was talking about.

'Elliott presents the breakfast show and then records a lot of the promotional adverts. Geoff does his radio show, then works out and types all the scripts for the other station features.'

I was still confused. He was telling me what everybody did. I already knew this.

'James makes the promos for all the other shows as well as doing his own show.'

Still nothing.

'And what do you do?' He looked at me blankly. 'I don't think you're pulling your weight.'

Now I got it and I was gutted. I had never been told before that I didn't pull my weight. I had always seen myself as a team player, and being told that I wasn't was devastating.

'Hang on, Steve, I flog my guts out every night on that show. I'm on the phone every day booking guests and getting prizes. I'm seeing movies and organising tickets to give away. I put my heart and soul into this radio show. I have increased the listener figures already in the first few months.

I work completely on my own and am often here till two o'clock in the morning sending out prizes to the listeners.'

Now what do you have to say to that, Mister Boss-man?

'But your show finishes at ten o'clock. You shouldn't be here till two in the morning. If it's taking you that long to work on your show, maybe you aren't working right.'

I was gobsmacked. How the hell do you get out of that one? I am working long hours, but I shouldn't be? This after he told me that I wasn't pulling my weight? It was at this point that I learnt two *very* valuable lessons.

STEVE MARTIN LESSON ONE:

If you are already at work when your boss turns up, he thinks you have been there working before anybody else gets in. This is good. If you turn up for work at five o'clock in the afternoon and the boss leaves at six, he only sees you for one hour. Therefore, he only sees you do one hour's work. This is bad.

STEVE MARTIN LESSON TWO:

Spending three hours on something while nipping out for a fag and making the odd phone call when really you could have done it in one hour … doesn't help either.

After this I made a point of getting into work very early at least one day a week. Even if I had nothing to do, it was just so the boss saw I was there. I also decided that staying at work after the show achieved nothing, as management weren't there to see it. So after I'd learnt my lesson, I'd finish the show at 10.00 p.m. and be in my car pulling out of the car park at 10.02 p.m. Thanks, Steve.

The Pulse was owned by the Metro Radio Group, based in Newcastle. It had recently purchased a few other stations in Yorkshire too. Now my boss Steve Martin was a big player in this group. However, he wasn't given the job as boss of all the Yorkshire stations. That honour was given to a man called Steve King. I always thought this put my boss's nose out of joint. We would occasionally talk about it, and as much as he said he didn't mind, I think he hated having to answer to somebody he didn't particularly like. Often the suits from the group would meet up somewhere in Yorkshire and my boss Steve Martin would tip me off.

'Now remember, Chris, I took a risk giving you this job. All the bosses will be tuned in tonight on their way to the hotel for this meeting tomorrow, so make us look good. Don't give these guys any ammo to have a go at you. There are some people just waiting to say "I told you so" when it comes to you.'

'What do you mean?' I asked. I was a bit of an idiot sometimes.

'I mean that some people in this group want you to fail. You're very young and doing things no other DJ does on these stations and you're making it work. They don't like it because you're kind of making them look bad. They're waiting for you to mess up.'

It was an interesting conversation that would come back to haunt me several months later.

I was due to present the New Year's Eve show. I had recently agreed my new contract with a bit more money; it was starting in about a month's time. I had organised so much stuff for that show I even wrote a page-by-page script of what I was going to do. A few weeks before I'd had a random audition for the television programme, *The Big Breakfast*. I had kept the TV script for it and decided it would look cool if I had a script for my New Year's Eve show that looked just like it. What a loser! I gathered a group of friends together in the studio for a nice party atmosphere and off we went. I started the show by singing a version of 'Panic' by the Smiths, featuring the legendary line 'Hang the DJ'. We had a load of callers on air having parties at their houses and all was going well. Then I told the story of how I got the job at the radio station, and how a few years before I had sent a tape to the old boss but didn't even get a reply. So I called him a miserable old sod.

One day in early January 1994, I got called in to see my boss Steve. He told me that a complaint had come in, it was serious, and that I should leave the building immediately and come back the next day. I had no idea what it was about and didn't feel the need to hang around.

The next morning I went back to work and sat in my boss's office. In there was my boss Steve Martin and the Yorkshire regional boss Steve King. They also had a secretary person in there taking notes. It turned out that the ex-boss had complained about my comments on New Year's Eve and that this was a very serious problem. I had slandered him. Or defamed him, they weren't quite sure, but they were sure it was serious enough to fire me there and then. Seriously. I was being fired for saying something very tame about a boss who didn't even work there any more. My boss Steve Martin looked sheepish throughout the whole thing. I remembered my conversations with him and knew that this was a load of bullshit. So I decided to say so. Calmly and professionally. I explained I thought this stank of other people trying to get me off the air because they were jealous their stations weren't getting the same results that I was. I looked Steve in the eye and asked him to remember what he had told me about other people being out to get me. Then the other boss decided to chip in.

'Chris, it's not like that at all. It's as simple as—'

I wasn't going to let him finish.

'I DON'T EVEN WANT TO TALK TO YOU,' I said. I didn't look
at him. I just pointed, and kept my eyes directly on my boss. The guy I
expected to look out for me.

'You said to me that this is what they wanted to happen. That they were
waiting for me to slip up. You know that this isn't even serious. You've just
given me a new contract. If I were that dangerous, why would you have
done that?'

Slimy Boss chipped in: 'Chris. it really isn't—'

'I'M NOT EVEN TALKING TO YOU SO SHUT UP!'

'Steve, this is bullshit and you know it's bullshit. Looks like I finally slipped
up. And how quick they were to pounce.'

With that, I stood up and walked out.

I felt as though I had stood my ground and left that office with my head
held high. I walked past a few of my colleagues in the office who just
looked at me. Elliott saw me and asked what was going on. I told him
I had been fired. He just looked back at me. I kept my head up and
walked straight to my car. Got in, drove round the corner, and then cried
my eyes out.

FUCKING HELL. I'VE JUST BEEN FIRED!

It was such a horrible feeling. I had no idea what to do. Nothing. I drove
home numb, not knowing what the hell was going on. Fired from my job
that I really loved.

When I got home my friend James Cridland called me straight away and insisted on coming over and taking me for a pint. What a top lad. He later informed me that a few weeks afterwards he saw the ex-boss in his local pub one night and went over to have a go at him about me getting fired. The guy didn't know anything about it and told James that somebody at the radio station had contacted him and suggested he complained about what I had said.

Later that week, the radio station sent me a copy of the minutes of the two meetings I had. It was bullshit. They contradicted themselves so many times that it was obvious it was all rubbish. So I went to see a media lawyer in London to see if there was anything I could do. Turned out the lawyer knew Steve King from years ago. Oh fucking great, I thought to myself. However, the lawyer insisted that if any wrong had been done, then he would act on it. He took one look at the notes and told me that my firing was indeed unfair and that he would be only too happy to go ahead with action. His words filled me with relief. Although what he said was nice to hear, it was enough. There wasn't much else I could do. Taking the Metro Radio Group to court at the age of nineteen would have been career suicide. Whether I won or lost, who the hell would hire me after that? I decided to do nothing about it and try to move on. It was all a big fucking mess, and I was out of work.

Incidentally, after I was fired from the Pulse, they moved James onto my show, and then kicked me in the teeth with another one.

THEY KEPT THE FUCKING NAME OF THE SHOW!

I got fired, so they just dropped my name from the 'Evening Bit' and carried on. Bastards.

10

BEING OUT OF WORK ... IS HORRIBLE

I t's a strange feeling when you get fired, especially if it's out of the blue. One second you're presenting your show and trying your best to be different and individual. The next, you're sitting on your arse at home wondering what the hell happened. After the Pulse fired me I didn't really know what to do. Now I *never* thought that it was all over. I always knew that I'd get another job; it was just a matter of where, and more importantly when. I did the usual thing of feeling sorry for myself and doing nothing during the day and drinking every night with my mates who hated their jobs anyway. Then I decided to get off my arse and do something about it.

I would set my alarm every morning, get out of bed and get showered and dressed to be sitting at my desk in my bedroom in Leeds and start writing. Writing, I thought, was the key. I wasn't entirely sure what to write, but I thought that it looked good at the end of the day when you printed stuff out. It looked like I'd been creative. So I wrote lots of radio ideas and letters to other radio stations. I came up with funny sketches and song parodies. I even wrote a half-hour radio comedy about, surprisingly, a local radio DJ. It was called 'Next On The Line' and my idea was to sell it to Radio 4 and then have it made into a successful TV series. Sadly, though, it was shite. This has never been seen by *anybody*, and I would be quite embarrassed for it to be read now. But at the time, I thought I was doing well. I was out of

work, but I was writing a lot of stuff. Some of it was even quite funny.
Another thing I did was to keep convincing myself I was funny. Even
though I couldn't even get a job on a local radio station in York called
Minster FM (see what they've done there?), I had to keep reminding myself
that I was definitely going to get another job on the radio. I didn't have a
radio show of my own, but I could call in to one. So I did. This was when I
made my phone calls to Nick Abbot on Virgin Radio under different names
and voices. One of them was a Scouse-voiced fella who just said 'It's great'
about everything. After my first call on the air, Nick commented:

'I think we've just found ourselves a new star.'

That was great. I called a few more times and was known as 'It's great'
'cos I kept saying it in every call about everything. I even ended up in the
radio station for his last late-night show. I was visiting a friend of mine
called Wendy Lloyd, who I had been in Luxembourg with and who now
worked at Virgin. We had popped in to the station for Wendy to finish up
some work, and Nick was on the air, doing his last phone-in show. I called
up from a room near the on-air studio and said that I was in London,
drinking with some pals as I was upset they were cancelling his show.
As the conversation went on, Nick's producer and Wendy both saw me
sitting there chatting on the phone with a ridiculous Liverpool accent.
They looked at me, looked at each other and then realised that the regular
caller was me. The producer immediately signalled for me to run into the
studio live. Now, I had met Nick once before but I didn't think he'd
remember me and, hell, it was a chance to get on air and make some
decent radio, so I did. I told Nick to hang on as I was just getting another
beer. I placed the phone down and ran towards the studio door. As I burst
through, I screamed 'It's great' as loud as I could. Nick looked like I was a
terrorist about to blow his head off and take control of the station.

'Hiya, Nick, how are you?' I said in my awful Scouse accent.

'Oh my God,' replied Nick.

'Aren't you different in real life? I can't believe you're white.' I was on a roll.

'How the hell did you get in here?'

'I love your studio, Nick, it's great.' I was already running out of ideas. Plus Nick looked like he thought I was going to kill him.

In the nick of time, pardon the pun, Wendy and his producer ran in laughing. I think Nick twigged and remembered me from before as Wendy's friend. He looked relieved. Afterwards he told me he had no idea I wasn't a real caller, and he thought that it was funny. A nice result, but it didn't help me get a job.

Another reason why it's horrible being out of work as a radio DJ is that everybody else seems to be more rubbish than usual. I was still listening to the radio every day because I enjoyed it and, I suppose, to keep on top of what my potential competition would be when I eventually got a job. I think it's fair to say that most DJs on the radio are rubbish. This is for several reasons:

REASONS WHY DJs ARE RUBBISH

THE PAY IS RUBBISH.

With the odd exception, there isn't much money in radio. When I signed for the Pulse in Bradford it was for £15,000 a year. Six days a week, three to four hours a show, with three or maybe four weeks off if you're lucky. Also, because most DJs are technically freelance, there is no holiday pay. Bank holidays don't exist and don't even think about such phrases as 'double time' or 'days off in lieu'.

MANAGEMENT ARE RUBBISH.

Usually the boss of the radio station you are working for used to be a DJ, and probably not a very good one at that. They, however, believe they were the best thing on the radio since sliced bread. (Not that there's ever been a great DJ called Sliced Bread.) I have worked for at least one boss, whom I shall talk about later, who had been at the same radio station since day one. He was your typical 'And a very good morning to you on this lovely Tuesday morning and welcome along to the show' type of DJ. So when they hire new talent, they want them to do what they did. Anybody who seems a little different or creative either doesn't get the job, or, if they do, has any unique talent slapped right out of them.

A LOT OF DJs DON'T CARE.

Really, a lot of radio DJs fell into it by accident. To them it's not a skill or a privilege to be on the air, it's just a job. They go to work, talk pop-a-doodle-doo for a few hours and then go home. They do the same show day in day out and are quite happy with that. They normally don't like the music they play and haven't been to a live music gig since seeing Dollar in 1984.

DJs ARE STUPID.

Trust me. I have worked in professional radio since I was sixteen. I have worked on the air at seven radio stations with tens of DJs, and the majority of them are, quite frankly, thick as fuck. Your typical radio DJ is a scruffy, uncool, odd person. They wear trousers that even your dad wouldn't wear, they listen to Boney M CDs in the car on their journey into work and they holiday at the same caravan park in Eastbourne every summer. They are not interested in politics, news, music or indeed the real world. They like ITV sitcoms, wear Lynx Africa, 'cos it's cool and trendy, and think that DJs like me appeal to twelve-year-olds and council-estate dwellers. They think Radio 1 has never been the same since Dave Lee Travis resigned, although not for the same reasons that I do!

DJs ARE SCUM.

This is *so* true. In the world of commercial radio, it's all about the money. How little they pay you, and how much they can make and keep. The sales department is where the money is made, and that keeps the station going. The sales team sell the airtime to whoever they can and DJs end up doing a competition giving away fish fingers because the local fish-finger factory agreed to spend five thousand pounds on a month-long competition. The sales team are gods with company cars and paid-for holidays, and the DJs are merely the idiots who have to present a road show from the local summer fête or present their show live from a bus station because the bus company has also paid for a big promotion. God forbid that you want to do creative radio that actually costs money. Besides, you probably won't have time because you're giving away cough sweets as it's National Cough Sweet Week and the National Cough Sweet Association has also spent money on a big promotion.

So there you have it. You're paid £15,000 a year to present the mid-morning show on Radio Treehouse. You work six days a week and play the same songs every show. The highlight of your day isn't actually the show, it's flirting with Joyce in accounts who wears low-cut tops and was past her sell-by date about five years ago. Your neighbours get paid more than you and go on better holidays than you. You're probably divorced, going through some kind of mid-life crisis and are really looking forward to getting tickets to see Phil Collins in London, which is exciting in itself as you have only ever been there twice before. With all this in mind and a bank holiday to work again:

WHY THE HELL SHOULD YOU TRY AND HAVE THE BEST SHOW ON THE RADIO? YOUR LIFE SUCKS!

So every day I'm out of work, I'm listening to these guys, and it's killing me. I send out my tapes and my letters asking for work and sit and wait for the postman to send me a generic letter telling me that even though they don't have anything suitable for me at the moment, they will keep my details on file.

OH SHUT UP.

Where in the world does a company keep the details on somebody who isn't right to work there? Do they have huge warehouse-like rooms with row upon row of filing cabinets featuring the details of unsuitable employees? Why would they do that, and where *are* my details kept? Am I in the file with the other unsuitable DJs, just underneath murderers and mutes?

If you don't receive that letter, you get a semi-positive one asking you to keep in touch. This again I don't understand. Do they want postcards from my holiday? Then when you do call to speak to them about any work, they have no idea who you are and then tell you there isn't anything suitable at the moment. In the end I got a phone call from a radio station that was interested in me, so that positive letter *never* arrived.

It doesn't matter who turns you down, it only matters who gives you your next job. For me at that time, having been out of work for over three months, it was the best news ever. It was presenting the evening show, which I had just been doing at the Pulse, and it was five days a week instead of six. Bonus: the money was exactly the same, though I had to fight for it because they wanted to pay me £14,000 a year and said they couldn't afford £15,000. They seriously couldn't afford an extra thousand pounds spread over twelve months. And I'm going to work for this company. This was my introduction to probably the strangest radio station I have ever worked for. Ladies and gentlemen, may I introduce to you, the staff of Signal Radio in Stoke-on-Trent. The city that time forgot.

MY FAVOURITE GUESTS

MADONNA

A slight cheat this one, as Madonna never actually came into the studio. We did manage to interview her at the Brit Awards in 2006. For the past few years Radio 1 have had a studio set up backstage at the Brits. When the artists and stars come off the stage, they are brought to a kind of press 'rat run' where all the press anxiously await the big stars. We have our studio right at the front of this mess and as the stars enter we are asked whether or not we want to interview them. Word comes through to us that we might have an interview with Madonna.

'Yeah, right. Whatever,' says me.

'Madonna's not going to come in here,' said Comedy Dave, referring to our tiny, hot, makeshift studio. Then the news is that she's not doing *any* interviews. Followed almost immediately by the news that Madonna is now *definitely* doing an interview with us. It's all so bloody complicated. Now, at this point I had never really wanted to interview Madonna. The reason for that was simple: I thought she'd be a stuck-up bitch. I'm sure she can be lovely but Madonna always struck me as a guest who would be hard work for me to interview. I doubt very much that she would find us amusing and our senses of humour are probably too different. Once again, I find myself being very wrong.

By the time she walks into the studio, all the team, including myself, are very excited. She says hello to everybody and then I get introduced to her.

'Hello. How are ya?' is my brilliant opening line to one of the sexiest women on the planet. And she is very sexy. She's smaller than you imagine but incredibly sexy. Her breasts look amazing through her outfit, and generally the consensus is: Madonna is one sexy fucking woman!

'Hullo. How are ya?' replies Madonna in a mock northern accent. 'Where are you from?'

'I'm from Leeds, luv.' The accent getting slightly stronger.

'Leeds, oh I know Leeds,' Madonna replies. I'm sure she doesn't know Leeds as well as I do, but this is hardly the time to quiz her on Temple Newsam House, the Merrion Centre or the development round the Royal Armouries. We begin the interview, and immediately I felt very comfortable with her. It began very silly and increased in silliness as it went on. It was very funny, and Aled, who is a massive Madonna fan, said he had never heard an interview with her quite like it. It was just a funny, bizarre interview, and to explain how bizarre it was, within minutes Madonna and I were screaming at each other to 'fuck off', and laughing out loud. The unedited version of that interview is knocking around the internet somewhere, but suffice to say from that moment on I was in love with Madonna. I would *love* to get her into the studio one day for a proper chat, so just in case you're reading this, love, would you like to come into my show one day? If not, then you can fuck off!!

I LOVE MADONNA. (And most certainly 'would'!)

In no particular order, here are some more of my favourite guests from my Radio 1 shows.

NOEL GALLAGHER

I think Oasis are bloody brilliant. Noel has been a regular guest on the show for the past few years, despite never actually coming into the studio. We've met many times socially and he has been on the show maybe the most out of all my guests. We have even interviewed him for Euro 2000, Euro 2004 and most recently the World Cup 2006 in Germany. He is always honest, funny and a good laugh. Even at Christmas, which he hates by the way.

OZZY OSBOURNE

He's only been in the studio once, but I loved Ozzy. He was incredibly funny, alert and fascinating to talk to. To some guests I could just keep on talking and talking, and Ozzy is one of those. His life is amazingly interesting and his voice just makes me smile.

PINK

I love her. I think she is brilliant. Comedy Dave and I always joke about me fancying her, despite the fact that she looks like a bloke. This statement I find very offensive, as Pink to me is a beautiful, attractive woman. Granted she could probably squeeze you to death with her thighs, but I think she's gorgeous. We flirt when she appears on the show, and I think that secretly, deep down, Pink is a bit of a chubby chaser and fancies a bit of me too. Oh, she's also funny and talented and all that stuff.

WILL YOUNG

From the first time he came in to see us, during *Pop Idol*, I have liked Will. He makes me laugh and I make him laugh. I remember talking about him being openly gay and that during his version of 'Light My Fire' he should change the line to: 'Come on, Brian, light my fire.' We got a lot of complaints about that because the listeners thought, by his obvious silence afterwards, that Will was offended. He wasn't being silent, he was trying to stop himself from laughing out loud, and was waving his hands round to get me to stop talking and play a record. It's always a good listen when he's on the show and he's always up for a laugh. That was, until the last time he came into to see us, when he was a bit moody and quite hard work. Rachel has said that unless he improves, he isn't coming back. That's show business for you.

50 CENT

A lot of US rap acts can be pretentious, wanky tossers who have their head stuck so far up their arse that if they sneezed it would come out of their bottom. Luckily, 50 Cent breaks the mould and is very funny. He plays along and has a great sense of humour. We met him in New York and I asked him if he would buy Leeds United. I have asked various guests this over the years, but for a brief second I thought he might ... He didn't.

RICHARD ASHCROFT

When he came on the radio show, everybody raved at what a brilliant guest he had been. We got thousands of text messages that morning, and after the show in the office everybody was saying how brilliant the interview was. Personally, I thought it was just all right. However, I was impressed when he brought his guitar out of nowhere and asked what we'd like him to sing. Some solo artists get very weird and pissed off if you ask them to play something from a previous band. Dave didn't give a shit about that and blurted out a request for 'Lucky Man'. Thirty seconds later, Rachel, Dave and myself are sitting in a studio watching Richard Ashcroft play and sing an amazing acoustic version of the Verve's classic. He was great and is welcome back any time – as long as he brings his guitar!

PATSY KENSIT

This woman has been a crush of mine for years. Since her days as a pop star in the band Eighth Wonder, when she was fit, to being an actress in *Lethal Weapon 2*, when she was really fit. Even running round *Emmerdale* farm, she still looked fit. When she came on the show it turned out she was a massive fan. She listened every day and could name everybody on the show, including Aled. During the interview we started talking about some show T-shirts we'd had made up which I wanted her to try on so I could see how she looked. We ran out of time and she had to leave to catch a train, but she promised me she would take a picture later and send it to me. Yeah, right, of course she would. Well, she did. Later that afternoon I got a text message with a picture of Patsy Kensit wearing an 'I HATE CELEBRITY TARZAN' T-shirt. And yes, she still looked fit. She is one of the highest-rated guests we've had on the breakfast show. Funny and fit would be my description.

ANDI PETERS

Star of children's TV and friend of Ed the Duck (not Gordon the Gopher, as everybody thinks), Andi has been a good friend of mine for the last few years. He loves being on the show slightly more than even I do. I have never known a person with a bigger ego than me! He's always funny on air and never gets annoyed when I cut him off, which is every time he's been on the show. And still he doesn't learn. Bless him!

SIMON COWELL

Fascinating man. He had no idea who I was when he walked into the studio. He does now, and has occasionally even heard the show!

ROBBIE WILLIAMS

I had been asking him to come on the radio show for years but he always whinged that he hated live radio and got nervous. I have a very strange relationship with Robbie, which has included being invited to his house in Los Angeles, and having to defend myself to him because he heard I was slagging him off on air. Me? Do a thing like that? For once and for all I will give my honest opinion of Rob, despite the fact that he will probably hate it and never talk to me again. I like him, he's a very likeable guy, but he's so fucking full of issues that it's almost impossible to talk to him. I've known him on and off for about six years, and even I don't know what relationship we have. He seems so honest in one conversation and then extremely guarded in another. Unless you're Jonathan Wilkes or Ant and Dec, you can't get near him. When you do, Robbie is always lovely and pleasant, and treats you like an old friend. When he finally came on the radio show he was fine. However, when I walked into the 'live lounge', the room where we hold our guests until they're ready to be brought into the show, he casually said 'Hi', as if he'd seen me the night before.

'Balls to that, mate, give us a hug,' I said as I flung my arms round him. Then, when he's on the show, he's all, 'Yeah, we're mates, me and you.' Very odd. Despite that, the guy is brilliant to interview 'cos you just don't know what mood he's going to be in. And if you're reading this, Rob, I'd like a hug next time we bump into each other. Failing that, pop round for a cup of tea. I've even got Earl Grey.

MATT LUCAS AND DAVID WALLIAMS

Both of them are brilliant. Matt is easier to talk to than Dave, but that's because Dave is usually either accusing me of flirting with him, or he's flirting with me! I always love the surreal tangents we end up on when they come on the show. Matt has a brilliant memory for all things kitsch and naff. I'm sure he remembers the theme tune to *Duty Free*.

CHRIS MARTIN

Came on the show the day before the Brit Awards and seemed so fucking out of it. He looked as if he was wearing the same clothes he had worn for the last day or two, and the night after we met him, he *still* seemed to be wearing the same clothes on TV at the Brits. I know he doesn't drink or do drugs, and I don't think he ever should. He was so wired when he came in to us, it was really odd. He was surreal and generally strange. But, as usual, I thought it made brilliant radio. Even though I maintain that I do not lead a celebrity-filled life, Chris and his wife Gwyneth are my neighbours, and occasionally, and I stress occasionally, Chris and I will chat over the gate.

DREW BARRYMORE

The legendary interview with her isn't actually that bad. It was a simple misunderstanding. I had always fancied Drew Barrymore and was excited when she was booked to come in *live* one morning. I remember thinking that she and I would bond and get on like a house on fire. Guess what? I was wrong. I went overboard flirting with her and it went down like a fart in a crowded lift. I wouldn't give up and kept on at her, thinking that eventually she would come round to my sense of humour. Wrong again. In the end she left thinking that I was weird and has, so far, never even been back in the Radio 1 building, let alone on our show. Sad.

WILL SMITH

Now this guy is a real star. I first met him a few years ago when he came in to the afternoon show. He was brilliant. He knew exactly how to handle us and there was a lot of laughter during the interview. His entrance was slightly odd in that the security guard on duty that afternoon brought him straight down to the studios without calling us first to let us know he had arrived. Then he was ushered into the wrong studio and had to walk through the door on his own to find us mid-link live on the air.

'Hey, it's Will Smith,' I proclaimed.

'Hey, what's happening, Chris? I've been looking for you guys all over the place. You got a lot of studios down here, man,' screamed Will.

He dived straight into it and was excellent. A lot of famous people come on the show and are either nervous or reluctant to join in and have some fun. It makes it difficult for us to try and keep the pace of the show going and keep everybody tuned in. Will Smith is so easy to interview – if you can't get anything decent out of *him*, you may as well hang your headphones up for good. After the interview he told us he was having a party at Planet Hollywood and we should pop down and say hello. We didn't need asking twice, so later that evening we walked into Planet Hollywood and waited to say hello to him. As the evening went on it got busier and busier, so Dave and I decided to have one more drink and then go home. As we were leaving we saw Will sitting in the corner of a little VIP section, so we went over to say goodbye.

'Hey, fellas, thanks for turning up. Come and join me for a drink,' he yelled.

Well, Dave and I are nothing but polite, so we stayed for a drink with him. He told us how much he enjoyed the show and that he would definitely come on again. This we hear a lot with US stars and it usually means nothing. However, a few years later when he was promoting the movie *Hitch*, Will came back to the show to hang out with us. He genuinely seems like a nice guy, and he is welcome back any time.

11
STOKE–ON–TRENT – NICE WHEN IT'S FINISHED

I had a new job. It was Monday to Friday presenting the evening show on Signal One in Stoke. Like most radio stations it used to broadcast on FM and AM, but then split into two services with pop music on the FM side and oldies on the AM side. The FM side was named Signal One and the AM service was, of course, Signal Gold. It was 1994, when pop music ruled the charts. Eternal, Michelle Gayle, Let Loose and Take That, who would turn from being just another boy band to being taken seriously by everybody with the release of the brilliant pop record 'Back For Good'.

I drove from Leeds down to the radio studios one day to confirm everything and sign the contract. For once I wasn't late. I even had time to find the station then have a bit of a look at the city centre. I drove past the radio station on my right and kept going. I passed the disused car wash on the left. I passed the boarded-up cinema on my right and turned back at the old shopping centre. I parked in the car park at the radio station and walked round to the front doors. It was at the end of a street of what looked like student housing. By the time I'd walked into the reception, I had a good idea of the kind of place Stoke was. The boss of the station was a man called John Evington. I was brought into his office and we started to chat.

'Did you find the place OK, Chris?' asked John.

'Yeah, I did, quite easily actually. Even had time to have a look round.'

'Oh great. Did you find the town centre?' he went on.

'Well, I'm not sure. I passed a disused cinema, a car wash and lots of boarded-up shops but don't think I found the actual city centre itself.'

'What? Just up the road here? Oh no, that is the city centre!' He looked quite proud of it, almost as though he'd made it himself. And, to be honest, it did look that way.

'Oh right. That *is* the city centre. I didn't realise.' What was I meant to say? It's a shit hole?

'What did you think of it?' Jesus, maybe he *did* make it himself.

'Well, I'm sure it'll be cracking when it's finished.'

He looked at me with a bemused expression on his face. 'What do you mean by that?'

I knew from this point on that John didn't get my sense of humour. Less than a year later, I would be proved right.

Signal Radio was a very odd place to work. First, the receptionist, Hilda, had *the* strongest Stoke-on-Trent accent ever. Now I suppose we all speak in a funny accent of some kind, but this was weird. For a start, everybody in Stoke calls everybody 'duck'.

'Hiya, duck. You all rite?' Odd. They don't sell fish and chips, they sell fish and *cheps*.

Secondly, in the reception area was a flight of stairs. Halfway up the stairs, on a balcony, was a fake beach, complete with sand. The reason for this I never found out. The station itself was very local radio. A lot of the staff had been there from the start, and I don't think their attitudes to work, or indeed style, had ever changed. The managing director looked like Chewbacca from *Star Wars*. John, my new boss, was the first voice ever heard on the station, and he still sounded *exactly* the same. He was a strange man, pleasant enough, but stuck somewhere between 1984 and 1988.

The on-air talent was a strange mix of DJs. It seemed like we were all either fired from our last jobs or couldn't get a job anywhere else. Spence MacDonald on the breakfast show had been fired from his last job. Mark Williams on the afternoon show was desperate to get out and couldn't. The whole station was like a DJs' refuge. On the AM service was a guy called Mel Scholes. He was a local legend who, in the old days, used to do a show called 'Pub of the Week' where they would broadcast live from a different pub every Sunday. In the office, there weren't enough desks to go round for the DJs, so we all had to share. All of us, with the exception of Mel. He had his desk tucked in the corner. Full of mail and photos and various bits and bobs. Strange, really, 'cos I never saw him sit at it. To me this was fair enough, as he'd been there since for ever and was a local hero. I sat at his desk once, though, as I needed to use the phone. On it were loads of fan letters and photo requests. A quick glance at them showed they were all from fans of about five to seven years old! Whether he left them lying there to make himself look more popular, or he really hadn't used his desk for years, I never did find out. Mel died a few years ago, but ask anybody from Stoke over the age of forty, and they'll remember him as the funny Scholesy from 'Pub of the Week'.

My first show on a new station is always a mixed affair. I will be all charged up and ready to go, itching to impress the listening audience and get them on my side. Mark Williams was on before me; he was a great bloke. We became mates instantly and used to back each other up if one of us got depressed, which happened a lot at Signal Radio. So I started my first show and Mark left me to it. I looked at all the jingles in the rack and chose one to play after the first commercial break. It was called 'Cloud in the Sky'. The last advert finished and I played the jingle. A laser effect played with a voice that said:

'Not a cloud in the sky. Signal One.'

What the fuck does that mean? It was 7.15 in the evening. Not a cloud in the sky? How could you tell? It was pitch fucking black outside. Luckily, I never had to read the weather because it wasn't sponsored for the evening show. For the daytime shows it was sponsored – by a local windows company. The guy who ran it was called Alan Wilma and the company was called Wilma Windows. After the news *every hour* the jingle would play and the DJ would read the weather, as sponsored by Wilma Windows. Then there would be an advert for them too, and, of course, as it was local radio, Alan had to do his own voiceover. The guy again had such a strong Stoke accent that this was funny, though it wasn't meant to be. The music was a sound-alike of *The Flintstones* theme tune. As in Fred and Wilma. Genius.

'Hi, I'm Alan Wilma from Wilma Windows. Pop in and see us for your new windows, doors and conservatories.'

It really was a weird place to work.

The second-in-command boss was another odd bloke. He was called Terry Underhill, and as well as being the number two boss, he also presented the mid-morning show. He was fairly young, probably in his late twenties/early thirties. However, he *loved* the music of Barry Manilow and Gloria Estefan. The guy was unbelieveable. I swear he had no connection to the real world whatsoever. He had his own office and often invited me in to show me his latest record-company invite. He was always going down to London for a record-company gig, and he loved it. If you tried to have a conversation with him, he would interrupt you and show you his latest invitation. One afternoon I went in to talk about my show. I put my head round the door and asked if he had five minutes to talk about an idea I had.

'Sure, sure. Pop right in and take a seat.'

I sat down in his office.

'So, what do you wanna talk about?' he asked, sitting back in his chair.

'Well, I have an idea for the show, which I think will be brilliant. It would, however, need a bit of money so I can get some decent prizes, but it would be absolutely huge and I know everybody would talk about it. The idea is this: it's a competition that runs over a few weeks. We ask the audience to send us in ...'

As I'm talking, Terry reaches into his drawer and takes out a compact disc that's not in a case. He moves it up to his eye line ...

... AND STARTS TO PLAY WITH HIS HAIR IN THE REFLECTION OF THE DISC!

'Erm, Terry. What are you doing?' I asked.

'Go on, go on, I'm listening. A competition, right?' He just carried on fixing his hair, using the CD as a mirror.

'Right, well, erm, yeah, it's a big competition where we ask the audience to register with us. Then every night we give one listener a massive prize. You know, something like a free shopping spree or a gold disc from a top band or something.'

At this point Terry puts down the CD and starts to rummage round on his desk. I just keep talking.

'The twist is that we ask everybody else who's listening if they think the caller deserves the prize. If they don't think they deserve it, we take it back and give it to someone else. It's great 'cos it makes all the audience want to listen, even if—'

'Hey, do you know what this is?' Terry has found what he was looking for and he picks it up, using his hand to cover up what's written on it.

'What? No, I've no idea,' I said.

'Have a guess, have a guess!'

'Terry, I've no idea, I'm in the middle of a pitch to you about an idea for the—'

'Look, look!' He slowly moves his hand away from the piece of paper. 'It's an invite to a playing of the new Gloria Estefan album in London.'

I stared at him. My boss. The man who is meant to nurture me and guide me. Help me become the best broadcaster ever.

'Terry. Amazing as that is, I'm not really bothered.'

'Well, have you got one?'

'An invite to a Gloria Estefan album party? No, I haven't.' Who cared anyway?

'Well, I've got one. And it's in London, and the record company are paying for me to go on the train. How cool is that?'

'Honestly, Terry? It's not cool.' Now I wasn't the coolest guy in the world, but do me a favour. Gloria Estefan!

'Gloria Estefan's not cool? Well, that just shows how little you know about music, doesn't it?'

I couldn't believe it. This guy was my boss and he was getting all excited about Gloria fucking Estefan. Plus, he has a CD in his desk drawer that he uses as a mirror to check his fucking hair.

THIS NUMB NUTS IS IN CHARGE, FOR CHRIST'S SAKE!

I did make some pals at the station. As well as Mark, there was Spence MacDonald, who did the breakfast show. We got on very well. He had a wicked, camp sense of humour, which I enjoyed, and we would bitch about everybody, in a funny way of course. We also spent a lot of time drinking and coming up with ideas, only to realise the next day that we had been very drunk and the ideas were rubbish.

Richie Pask did the late show after me. He, too, was desperate to get out of there and find a better job. He lived in Birmingham and travelled up and back on the M6 every day to do the show. No wonder he wanted a better job.

Another pal I made was my next-door neighbour, Lee. I had found a house to rent through a letting agency in town. It was an OK house at the end of a close in the nicer part of a fairly dodgy area of Stoke. It had two bedrooms and a little garden at the back. The house belonged to a professional footballer. I won't name him, as I found out he was a *very* peculiar character. Within a few weeks he had called me up at the house to ask if he could have the rent money a few days early. I told him that I hadn't been paid myself yet and anyway I was on a direct debit with the letting agency so couldn't change the date. This wasn't the answer he wanted to hear and he quickly ended the call. A few days later I got a phone call asking for him. I said he didn't live here any more and the guy on the other end asked if I had a phone number for him. When I explained I didn't, the voice went very serious and said that when I saw him I was to tell him to call 'Vince' straight away. This man didn't sound like an old friend! Another time I came home to find a note through the door saying that they had turned up looking for Mr Footballer and that they would be back. At this point I knew it wasn't Real Madrid trying to get hold of him. One day he called me and asked if he could stay the night on the Saturday, as he would be in town. What a cheek! I explained that as I didn't know him and I was paying money to rent the house from him, it really wasn't a good idea.

Luckily, I didn't have any problems with my next-door neighbour. Lee was cool. He told me stories about Mr Footballer and confirmed my suspicions. One Monday afternoon I came back to the house from a weekend visiting Mum and Dad in Leeds. I put the key in the door but it wouldn't open. I gave it a push but it wasn't moving. I went and knocked on Lee's door.

'Oh, you're back already. Sorry, I didn't see you arrive,' he said calmly.

'Mate, I'm having trouble getting in my front door,' I said.

'Oh yeah, sorry, that was me. I took your lock out on Saturday.'

'Lee, why did you do that?' I asked.

'I'll explain in a minute. Let me get my tool bag and I'll put it back in for you.'

With the lock fixed and a cup of tea on the go, Lee explained.

By now I knew Mr Footballer was a 'bit of a boy'. I also knew that he sometimes wanted to 'pop in' and see his old place. With this in mind I used to bolt-lock the back door whenever I went away. On this particular Saturday, Mr Footballer called Lee to tell him that he'd be in Stoke that night. Lee asked where he was staying, and Mr Footballer told him he'd be staying at his own house next door because he knew I was away.

'Mate, you can't do that. Chris is paying rent money to live there. You can't just turn up and stay the night.'

'Listen. He's away for the weekend, so he'll never know. Besides, it's my fucking house and if I want to say there I'll stay there,' said Mr Dickhead Footballer.

Lee knew what this guy was like, and that he probably would turn up at the house, no doubt with some lovely lady in tow, let himself in, shag her in my bed, then leave. (Lovely guy!) So with this in mind, Lee took the lock out of my front door. About 2.30 the next morning, Lee woke up to hear banging outside. He looked out of the window to see Mr Footballer's car parked in the street, with a lovely lady sitting in the passenger seat, and Mr Footballer himself kicking the crap out of my front door trying to get it open. It's the usual story of a man trying to break my door down so he can shag a bird in my bed at the house that I'm renting from him.

WELCOME TO STOKE-ON-TRENT!

I finally got fired from Signal Radio. Well, I didn't get fired, I was 'dropped'. Apparently there is a difference. I'm not sure what it is. You lose your job and don't get paid any more. To me, it's the same. However, when I was 'dropped' by my boss John Evington, he assured me I wasn't being fired. He had called me in to explain that I had been turning into a 'shock jock' and he was very worried about it.

'I just don't know what to do,' he said.

'Well, John, I don't see myself as a "shock jock". I'm just trying to be different and entertaining.'

You see. A lot of people think I'm a bastard to deal with. I'm not. I'm also not stupid. When it comes to my work, I treat it as my business. I may speak on the radio like I don't care, but I do. It's the show; it's what I do. However, when I'm sitting in the boss's office, I talk to the boss like anyone would speak to a boss. Plus, I had a feeling what was coming, so I had to try and seem like a reasonable, rational human being.

'I've made a lot of decisions in my time as boss here. I don't want to make the wrong decision about you,' he whimpered.

'Then leave me to it, John. Trust me. I know what I'm doing. The listening figures are up and the show is really popular. If there's something you don't like on the show, tell me and we'll change it.'

'No, it's not that. It's … Well, I can't explain what it is. But I have written it down in this letter for you.' He passed me a letter but I didn't open it.

'John. You're the boss. Are you firing me?' Asking the obvious I know.

'No, I'm not. But I am going to let you go,' he said.

It's at this time that you have to quickly assess the situation. In the blink of an eye you have to cover every possibility and work out what the outcome will be. Was there a chance I could've talked him into keeping me? If there was, it was very slight. Was he definitely going to get rid of me there and then? Probably, yes. Well, in that case, I have nothing to lose.

'John, let me get this straight. You've written down in a letter why you're firing me because you can't explain it to my face. Is that correct?'

'No. I told you, I'm not firing you, but I am going to drop you,' he said.

'Oh, OK. Well, in that case …

… FUCK YOU AND STICK YOUR JOB UP YOUR ARSE, YOU SPINELESS BASTARD.'

And with that, I walked out of his office and went to the pub with Spence to contemplate what the hell I was going to do next.

PS. I never read the letter.

WRITING A BOOK

AND WHY I HATE JEREMY CLARKSON ... KIND OF

When I took the job on of writing this book, I thought it would be easy. I mean, look at the facts. It's only writing a few words. OK, there are 70,000 words, but how hard can that be, right? And it's also my favourite subject: me. Write a few words about myself, put in a few pictures and there you have it. Easy. As we say in the radio industry, a piece of piss.

WRONG!

I couldn't be more wrong, in fact. I'm so wrong that I find myself avoiding my editor, Claire. (I love the fact that I have an editor. Look at me, Chris Moyles, the author, with my very own editor!) She calls me and I don't call her back. I know it's wrong but I have no choice. Normally I love talking to her. She's a cute Irish girl. Nice voice too. It's nothing to do with her not being cool or anything. The reason I'm not calling her back is the fact that the publishers are expecting half of the book YESTERDAY! That's right, they want about 35,000 words.

AND I'VE ONLY WRITTEN 18,000.

Shite! I've been so busy thinking how easy the book's going to be to write, that I haven't written any of it. BOLLOCKS! Luckily, I have a holiday from work planned. A well-earned two-week break in the sun. I plan to go somewhere hot with Sophie and chill for ten days.

WRONG!

I have to write the flaming book. While Sophie sits on her arse in the sunshine, I have to sit here in the room and type into my little laptop at least another 17,000 words. But do not worry, readers. I have a plan. Or at least, I thought I did.

It's now the first evening of my holiday. It's 6.30 p.m. The sun is starting to set. Slowly disappearing into the sea. From my hotel room I can see it clearly. I have chosen a hotel that is quiet. I will swim and sunbathe as usual, tanning my big fat belly in the belief that if I'm brown I won't look so fat. What an idiot. Anyway, the plan is to retire to the room in the late afternoon and write. At the airport I bought some books to give me some well-needed inspiration. I thought that if I read what other people have written, it might get me all worked up into Super Writer mode. I bought a David Beckham book. Not that I thought he sat down and wrote it himself, but still it might help. You know, all them things about when he was a lad and all that shit. I know our careers are somewhat different – he is one of the best footballers of his time and I play records and talk shit for a living – but it's a start. At the very least it'll be an interesting read, I suppose.

The second book I bought was written by one Jeremy Clarkson. Now I've always liked Clarkson. I don't know much about cars but I've always found him amusing. Comedy Dave off the show used to think he was an arse. So much so that when we launched our website, we had a celebrity dartboard on it. You could choose the celebrity you hated the most, and throw darts at their face. I chose a few of the victims. I had Atomic Kitten, a band made up of some council-estate lovelies. Phill Jupitus, who hates me to this day. Jamie Oliver was also on there, but that was when everybody hated him, before he became all right. Dave made his own list. On that list was one Jeremy Clarkson. I must point out that since those days Dave has had a massive change of heart about Mr Clarkson. He now thinks he's funny too. Back then he thought he was an over-tall denim-wearing arsehead. But Dave is now mellower than he was in his early twenties and is a big fan. Sadly, however, Clarkson now thinks *I'm* an arse. I don't know whether this comes from what Dave used to say about him on air, or whether he's always hated me, but either way I don't believe he's a fan. I am, though, a fan of his, and I hoped I could steal from his book.

On the front of Clarkson's book, *The World According To Clarkson*, it reads:

OVER 500,000 COPIES SOLD

Now that's the book for me. I need inspiration to write my book, and it's going to come drenched in denim with shit hair. It's all so easy now.

WAYS IN WHICH JEREMY CLARKSON CAN HELP ME WRITE MY BOOK:

I read Clarkson's book.

I become inspired, like John Belushi in The Blues Brothers movie.

Write 17,000 words of award-winning material.

Send to Claire, my editor, to read.

She loves it.

I win the Booker prize.

WRONG AGAIN!

I open Mr Denim's book and read the following: 'The contents of this book first appeared in Jeremy Clarkson's *Sunday Times* column.'

WHAT?

You have to be kidding me. The first chapter was written on Sunday 7 January 2001. The next was written a week later, Sunday 14 January 2001. It dates from then all the way through until Sunday 14 December 2003. 2001 to 2003? I've got to write 17,000 words in ten days, and he wrote a book in three fucking years. That's not fair. I bet he's not on holiday tapping away on his laptop, which is probably better than mine anyway. Oh no. He'll be driving round in flash sports cars with no roof, the wind flowing through his shit hair, comfortable in the knowledge another bestseller is going to write itself over the next three years! Cut straight to me now. Sitting in a pair of ill-fitting shorts. Tapping away like some nerdy kid on a PlayStation game (I'm an Xbox man myself!) while my girlfriend walks up and down the room bored out of her head as it's now seven o'clock and I'm still writing. **On my holiday!**

THAT'S WHY I HATE JEREMY FUCKING CLARKSON.

That said, what I read wasn't bad, and he did inspire me to write about 1,000 words, so he's not all bad. **Thanks, Jeremy.**

12
FROM STOKE
TO MILTON
KEYNES

It's mid-1995, I'm twenty-one, and once again I find myself living at home with Mum and Dad. I don't mind being back here. Even though I've lived on my own in Luxembourg and the dizzy heights of Stoke-on-Trent, it's actually quite nice being back in my old room. Plus, since I've technically been fired again, I think Mum and Dad feel it too much to ask for me to pay for my 'board'. So I set myself the task of finding another job in radio. I know what to do by now, and I know it only takes one job before I'm back on track again. However, it's still a pain in the arse sending off demo tapes to bosses and then calling them day after day only to fail to get through.

I spoke to Paul Chandler and Mark Collins at Chiltern Radio in Dunstable, but they moaned about the money. This one was annoying, as it was for the evening show, 7 p.m. until 10 p.m., which I had done at the Pulse and at Signal. The Chiltern show was syndicated on four of their other stations in Milton Keynes, Bedford, Northampton and Gloucester. I wanted at least to stay on the same money I had been on before and I thought that £15,000 a year to broadcast on five separate stations at the same time wasn't exactly going to break the bank. For every commercial break, each station would filter off and play its own local adverts. Therefore, in theory, with each 30-second spot they were bringing in five times the money, from five separate commercials. I couldn't believe they were moaning about £15K.

'We're only paying £14K at the moment,' I was told.

'Well, in that case you're paying too little for a start, and I only want an extra thousand. I'm sure if you really want me you could split the money between the stations and it would only cost an extra £200 a year each,' I explained, thinking my brilliant business sense would make them see the light. They didn't and said they couldn't possibly go up to £15K. Luckily for me Mark Collins seemed to like what I did and said he would try his best to change their minds, and would keep in touch with me anyway. Unlike most bosses, he actually did, calling to update me on conversations with the management about me.

One morning, waiting to hear about my job, I got up early and had breakfast with Mum. I waved her off to work just as the phone started ringing. It was Clive Dickens. Clive was programme controller of the Capital Radio group, certainly the most exciting group of radio stations in the UK, with Capital FM and Capital Gold the flagship stations in London. To get a job on the air at Capital would be amazing. A dream come true for a DJ like myself. This could be the defining moment of my career.

'Chris, it's Clive Dickens.'

'All right, Clive, how are you?' I asked as if he were an old friend and not somebody whose arm I would chew off for a job.

'Yeah, all right. Listen, how's the work situation?'

Now this is a difficult one. Do I tell the truth and explain that once again I've been fired, giving the impression that maybe I'm a gamble to hire, or do I lie and tell him that I'm fighting off job offers as I'm such a sought-after broadcaster? Then again, I don't want to price myself out of the market and appear too cocky. I settle on the truth.

'Slow. Think there might be something going at Chiltern Radio but I'm just waiting to see if they can come up with more money.'

It was the right option to take.

'Chiltern? Good station, I worked there. Who you dealing with – Mark Collins?'

'Yeah, he's trying his best to get me for the evening show so I'm kind of hanging in there waiting to see what happens.'

'Well, I have something I want to run past you. It's not a presenting job, but I think you're the right man for it. We have a station down south called Power FM. The breakfast show is OK, but needs a good kick up the arse. It needs to be more exciting, with funnier bits in it. Basically it needs a bloody good producer who can bring a lot of fresh new ideas to it, and I thought of you.'

This was amazing. Clive Dickens was asking for *my* help. He's calling *me* to ask if I can help *him* out and turn his shite show into something brilliant. I was flattered. But it wasn't a presenting gig, and that's what I really wanted. I knew what I had to say.

'Clive, that is a very nice idea, and I'd love to go in there and sort it out for you, but I've got to be honest, I really want to do my own show and I think that's where my skills really lie.' I was out of work and turning a decent job offer down. God, I hope this is the right thing to say.

'I understand that. I just thought of you when we were discussing what we could do to improve the show, but you're probably right. You know what? Let's leave it and keep holding out for this Chiltern job. I'll be back in touch. Let me know how it goes.'

And with that, I had turned down my first ever decent radio job. The phone call wasn't the defining moment of my career, after all. Or if it was, I was in trouble …

However, sometimes in life things go your way, and in a few weeks I was all packed up and heading down to Milton Keynes to present the evening show on Chiltern Radio. For £15,000 a year.

Milton Keynes is a strange place to live. It's a town based on the American grid system and has about a hundred roundabouts. The directions from Leeds to my flat in Milton Keynes went like this:

> M1
>
> Get off at junction 14 and turn right.
>
> At the next roundabout, call it 'roundabout number 1', go straight.
>
> Carry on to roundabout number 16, then take a left.
>
> I'm at the end of that road on the right.

As I said, they have many roundabouts.

The radio station where I was initially based was Horizon Radio. A fairly bland semi-dance station with average DJs. I was there to present the 7 p.m. until 10 p.m. show simulcast on their other stations under the strapline of 'The Hot FM'. It was very early-90s-sounding radio with lots of laser zaps and American-style jingles.

The on-air studio was used all day, with a spare studio through the glass where I was to do my show from. This was also where they recorded certain adverts for the station. In those days I used to record a fair bit before the show, doing interviews with passing pop stars on their regional radio tours and phone calls with guests who couldn't be arsed to drive the fifty miles out of London. This, amazingly, caused me my first argument at the station. I knew that the advertising people were used to having the studio when they wanted as it was always free, but I was going to need studio time on a daily basis to record, so I asked what hours I could have it from.

'What hours? It doesn't work like that. We have access to that studio all day,' said the snotty advertising woman.

'I understand that,' I explained, 'but I need to record for the show, so how about I have it from four o'clock every afternoon? That gives you seven hours a day to get your stuff done.'

This seemed like a good deal to me, as it was mostly empty anyway, but as I was new I wanted to seem like a team player.

'No. We use that studio when we like. Emma [the previous evening show presenter] was never in there pre-recording so I don't think we need to set up any rota system. You can have it when we've finished with it,' said the tiny grumpy woman.

This pissed me off. Here I was, an amazing radio talent, about to light up their output with my own unique brand of radio, being nice to this stubborn bitch because she had plodded along there without any interruption. I had tried to be calm and professional and courteous to her, but she wasn't playing ball back. She needed to be taught.

'Listen, love. I have no idea how things have worked here in the past but this is how it's going to work now. That studio is mine to do the show. I need to prepare in that studio every day. I have offered you a solution but you're not being nice about it, so here's how it will work. Every day at four o'clock

I will go in there to do my stuff. If you haven't finished by then, then I'm afraid it's tough. Sorry it has to be like this, but it does. And if you have any problems with that, then I suggest you take your little company car down to Dunstable and speak with Mark Collins about it. All right, love?'

She looked at me in shock and eventually walked away.

SCORE: MOYLES 1 – NASTY ADVERTISING WOMAN 0

Things got better, to be fair, in Milton Keynes, and I was about to start enjoying myself when the news filtered through the building that we had been taken over – by the GWR Group.

This was a problem.

The GWR Group was nicknamed the McDonald's of Radio. They had come up with a format, and each station they took over was made to stick to that format. The breakfast shows consisted of a male DJ bantering with a female co-host. The rest of the day was four records in a row and lots of 'That was' and 'This is' links.

I WAS FUCKED.

They were *never* going to keep me on with my style. One of my features was called 'Throwing CDs at the Studio Clock'. I blindfolded myself and threw CDs from the back of the studio. A caller had to guess how many CDs hit the clock. I interviewed guests in my pants, and was generally not suited to the GWR style. Luckily for me, the big boss of GWR was called Steve Orchard and he had heard my show one night as they were doing the deal to buy the network.

'I like your style, but I think you should be a bit more adult. Could you adapt what you do and present the late show from 10 p.m. every night?'

I couldn't believe it. Not only was I not being fired, but he was asking me to take on the late show because he thought I could do something different with it.

'Your style is very individual and I like it. It wouldn't really be suited to our rigid format during the day, but I think at night it could really make an impact.'

Thank the Lord for Steve Orchard. I had been saved. After the GWR takeover we moved to Dunstable and I began working on ideas for a late show. I wanted lots of callers and silly stuff. This could be the start of a new era for me.

Goodbye kiddie evening show, hello grown-up late-night show.

Not many amazing things happened during my time here. Apart from my mate Jon flying through the air, that is, and meeting Steve Wright.

My mate Jon called me one morning to tell me he wasn't going to go into work that day because he had been involved in a car crash.

'Jesus, pal, are you all right?' I asked.

'Yeah yeah, I'm fine. Just a couple of scratches on my face and my right arm,' he replied.

'Oh right. So it wasn't anything serious then?'

'Well, a car hit me head on, spinning me into the path of an oncoming truck, which cut my car in half and sent me flying through the windscreen to land on one side of the road while the other half of my car landed on the other side.'

What do you say to that? The police said it must have been the sheer speed with which he went through the glass that kept him from being injured.

So, apart from Jon flying through the air on his way home, the other exciting thing was meeting legendary Radio 1 DJ Mr Steve Wright. He had been hired by GWR as a consultant. It meant they paid him a lot of money to teach crap DJs how to be slightly less crap. He came into the studios in Milton Keynes to meet all the DJs one by one. I was last on the list, as usual, but we got on straight away. We shared our thoughts on radio and what we liked and disliked about the industry. I remember he told me:

'All this GWR format radio is a bit boring. I can tell you're better than all that.'

'Well yeah, I like to think I am, but I still love their boring format radio,' I said.

'Do you really?' he asked, looking at me like I was insane.

'Yeah. Everybody on the station sounds the same, apart from me, which is great. If everybody was allowed to do something different, then maybe I wouldn't stand out so much. So in a sense, I need them on the air being boring and rubbish to make me sound fresher and more exciting.'

'I never thought of it that way. You're right.'

Here I was teaching Steve Wright about radio! We kept in touch after that first meeting and Steve ended up being a great supporter of mine, and still is. He helped me with lots of advice when I moved to London and eventually Radio 1. When I was offered the job at Radio 1, I met up with Steve for a drink and a chat. I told him that I was probably going to take the job. Steve pondered for a moment.

'Mmm, I suppose, yeah, it's probably the right thing to do,' he said, like some king giving royal permission.

'Well, shit, yeah, it's the right thing to do!' I yelled back.

'Yes, but Radio 1 isn't the place it used to be, you know. However, I do think you should take the job. I think you could be the last famous DJ to come out of that building.'

I remember thinking it was an odd thing to say, but maybe he was right. Who knows? Besides I'm not even there yet, I'm still living in Milton Keynes in 1996, so let's get back to that story 'cos I want to leave there as soon as I can!

'The Late Bit', as I called the show, was going really well. I was hardly setting the world on fire, but with only thirty-five miles or so to London from the Dunstable studios I was getting nearer and nearer to my dream job, whatever that would be. It was at Chiltern that I started to call myself 'The Saviour of Late-night Radio'. This was a play on Howard Stern's 'King of all Media' title, which he had made up for himself. Like Howard's, my silly nickname has stuck with me. Even now in the national press I'm described as 'the self-proclaimed saviour of Radio 1'. I must admit: I quite like it! So the show was going fine, and then one day I got a letter from Clive Dickens at Capital. He explained that he had been keeping an eye on me since I got the job at Chiltern Radio and he wanted me to send him down a fresh tape of the show. I wanted to keep him hanging for a bit, you know, to make them want me even more, but my flatmate Richie Pask, who'd left Signal Radio in Stoke and was working in a local nightclub, answered the phone one day to Clive's PA and told her that I was trying to be cool about it all but he would make sure a tape was put in the post in the next twenty-four hours. Cheers, pal!

Clive eventually called me to a meeting at Capital Radio's studios in London. Word came through that they were going to offer me a show at their station Power FM in Southampton, the station where I had previously turned down the producing job. I knew that it was London I wanted but I thought it would be a start to get in with this company, so I headed to London all excited.

After a year of living in Milton Keynes, and all the work I had done in Leeds, Luxembourg and Stoke-on-Trent, I finally started to think that I was on my way to London. I thought it might even happen in just a few more years. Once again, I was wrong.

13

THE DREAM JUST GETS BETTER

walked into the reception at Capital Radio in London in June 1996, buzzing. It's weird, because I always knew I would eventually make it to London, at the same time as being convinced it would never happen. But there I was, sitting in the reception of this legendary radio station. And it really was legendary. The station had been number one in London for years and showed no signs of slipping. As much as I was excited, I didn't really want the job in Southampton. It was Capital I desperately wanted. I played over and over in my head what I'd say if they did offer me the Power FM job. I decided I would take the risk of saying it was Capital I was after. Maybe they would see this as rude, but maybe they would see it as ambitious. Either way, I knew I had to say something; I just wasn't sure what it would be. I suppose I would find out sooner or later.

After a while I was called up by a PA, who greeted me with one of the funniest and most unprofessional openers ever.

'Hi, you must be Chris?' she asked with a beaming smile.

'Yes, I am. Pleased to meet you,' I said as I offered her my hand.

'You too. Come this way and I'll show you to Clive's office.'

We began walking up the stairs and then all of a sudden she said, 'So you must be very excited about coming to work for us then, Chris?'

I didn't even hesitate.

'Well, actually I'm only here for an interview. They haven't offered me anything yet, but thanks for the tip-off.'

Her face went white. 'Oh no. Well, forget I said anything.' She looked embarrassed.

I just smiled because I thought they were going to offer me the Power FM job anyway, so I began to run through in my head a few more ways of convincing them to think about me for Capital instead.

Inside the office, the meeting took a very casual form. Clive Dickens sat behind the desk with Pete Simmons, the controller of Capital FM. We ended up eating ice creams, of all things, and chatting for about an hour or so about radio, what I liked and disliked and how my style would fit in to their sound. As we talked, the radio was tuned to Heart 106.2, a competitor in London.

'OK, Chris. How are you on taking advice?' said Clive.

'It depends what it is.' I was such a cocky twat.

'Well, here's an example. Let's say you've made a joke about McDonald's on your show. Now McDonald's spend a hell of a lot of money with us on all our radio stations. If I told you not to mention McDonald's in a negative way, what would you do?' They both looked at me.

Straight away I answered. Remember I was a cocky twenty-two-year-old: 'I'd say that I wasn't allowed to mention McDonald's on the air and that my boss had given me a bollocking.'

Clive actually sighed out loud; Pete just looked at me and asked me why I would do that.

'It's simple. I would say that you had told me not to mention McDonald's on the air because they spend a lot of money on the radio station. Then I would explain that it's silly to try to stop me mentioning them because everybody loves hearing the word McDonald's. Even the mention of McDonald's makes you think of a Big Mac and large fries, or a strawberry milkshake and a burger. The more I mention it, the more you're thinking about it. You know what? If you're in your car now, drive to the nearest McDonald's and buy something. I know you fancy one, 'cos so do I. Go to the drive-through window, order whatever you like and tell them that Capital FM just told you to go and treat yourself to a McDonald's.'

They both looked at me in silence. I wasn't sure if this would work.

'After that, hundreds of people in London would do just that. The word would get back to head office and I guarantee that McDonald's would be on the phone the next day spending even more money advertising on my show.'

Again, they both looked blankly at me. After a few more seconds of silence, Pete said, 'What we meant was if we asked you not to say something about an advertiser, would you mind?'

'Oh, right. No, I wouldn't really be bothered. But I thought you wanted a creative answer.' I felt like an idiot, but also slightly proud of my marketing speech.

Then it came to why I was there. Clive started off the speech that would change my life.

'Chris, we like what you do. We think you are a unique broadcaster. All the way through this chat we've had Heart 106.2 playing in the background, and not once have they made any of us stop and listen. That's not what we want here. We want the radio to stand out, and that's what you have. You have the ability to make people stop what they're doing and listen to what you're saying. Which is why we'd like to offer you a job –'

This was it, crunch time. If they said Power FM, I was ready to argue with them about my place in the London market.

'– a job, here at Capital –'

SHIT THE FUCKING BED!

I'm being offered a job at London's number-one radio station.

' – six days a week, a one-year contract –'

OH MY GOD.

This was real. I couldn't believe it.

'– twenty-two thousand pounds a year –'

WHAT?

Clive continued but I didn't hear what he said.

I'M THIS GREAT BROADCASTER THEY DESPERATELY WANT, AND I'M ONLY WORTH £22K A YEAR?

I was shocked and actually a little bit annoyed. I thought if I made it to London it would be my payday. It's never just about the money, but I thought that after an hour of talking to me, when they knew they really wanted me, to offer me only a few thousand pounds more than I was now on at Chiltern bloody Radio was an insult.

'And the money is negotiable, right?' I asked Clive.

'Why would the money be negotiable? No, it isn't.' He didn't flinch.

'Well, to be fair, if I am this great talent you really want, then I think I'm worth more than twenty-two thousand a year, Clive.'

Pete went silent and looked at Clive, who seemed annoyed that I hadn't just bitten his arm off and kissed his feet.

'Well, if you're not happy with that,' said Clive, looking very pissed off, 'then I'll tear the contract up right now.'

I got the feeling that he had been expecting me just to take it and didn't like my money talk.

'Clive, don't be silly. This is what we do. You offer me a fee; I try and up the fee. It's simple radio business,' I explained. We talked back and forth for a few more seconds.

'Why don't you go away and think about it?' he said.

'And why don't *you* go away and think about it too?' was my brilliant reply.

So there it was. I had been offered a dream job on arguably one of the world's most exciting radio stations, and I left the building furious and deflated. I called home straight away and Dad answered.

'Well, not good then?' He could tell by the sound of my voice.

'Actually, they offered me a job on Capital FM in London. Twelve-month contract, six days a week,' I told him.

'That's what you wanted, wasn't it? So what's the problem?'

'Twenty-two thousand a year, Dad.'

He knew. Dad has always been a good judge of money and worth. He said I should think about it over the weekend, but if it is really what I want, then I should take it and let the big money come later. He's a wise man, my dad.

I thought about it and realised that I was fighting a losing battle and I should just take this amazing job offer, and start making the show work for London. I called Clive and told him I was in. And that he should expect at least to pay me a Christmas bonus!

Let me quickly explain why I did what I did. I knew I wasn't earning a lot of money, and after this job offer I knew I had an act that one of the biggest commercial radio stations in Europe wanted. This comes at a price. It's all part of the game. They were hoping I would just take the offer and be grateful. Now I couldn't wait to take the job, but I needed them to know that this is my business and that I am more than just a gob on a stick. I believe Clive saw me as more than some jobbing disc jockey, and we had a great relationship during my time at Capital. I got a pay rise in the end. I officially put it down to my brilliant work and not the fact that I saw something that I shouldn't have seen and then coincidentally was given a pay rise … Can't say more about it than that!

Capital FM was a huge station. Dominating London radio, it was untouchable. It had slipped slightly in the ratings but was still the city's number-one station. The guy who ran the whole thing was a radio legend by the name of Richard Park. He went on to be a judge on BBC1's *Fame Academy*, but, trust me, this did nothing to show what kind of a brilliant and frightening boss he was. He ran Capital like the Godfather ran the Mafia. Everybody and I mean everybody, with the exception of Chris Tarrant, was nervous around him. He was Scottish, tall and very scary. I got told a story by a friend of mine called Clare Ashford about how unpredictable he was.

'How was the show today, Clare?' he asked one day as she passed him in the corridor.

'Yeah, it was great, thanks, Richard.'

'Great? They're never great. Remember, lady, that there's always room for improvement.' And with that, he walked away.

The next week Clare had finished her show and was walking through the office when Richard walked past.

'How was the show today, Clare?' he asked.

'I think it went well, Richard, but there's always room for improvement,' she replied with a smile.

'If there's room for improvement, what the fuck are you doing working on my radio station? It should always be the best.'

And with that, he walked off again. Typical Richard Park. Luckily I always got on well with him and never had a row. The nearest I came to a telling-off was when I was called into his office to be told that a feature I did needed to be taken off the air.

'The first week you did it, it was OK,' he said. 'The second week it was boring. The week after that it was just getting tedious, and last night when I heard it it just sounded awful.'

'OK, I get the message, you thought it was shit,' I said.

Richard looked at me with a straight face and said, 'I never said it was shit. It just wasn't very funny, and I don't think you'll be doing it again, will you?'

I never did.

The line-up of DJs on the station was amazing. Chris Tarrant was king, presenting the breakfast show. He was paid an absolute fortune and was on something silly like fourteen weeks' holiday a year. Not surprising, really, as he single-handedly made the station a fortune back in advertising and revenue. He was very nice to me when I joined. As a joke I had told Clive Dickens that I would only sign the contract if I got signed pictures of Chris Tarrant and Doctor Fox. One day I looked in my mailbox and found a signed picture of Chris Tarrant. I saw him a week later.

'Did you get your picture?' he asked calmly.

'Yes, thank you,' I squeaked, slightly embarrassed at the thought of the boss asking him to sign a picture to their latest DJ signing.

After Tarrant on the breakfast show, it was a crazy mix of other legendary DJs, including Pat Sharp, Mick Brown, David Jensen and Doctor Fox.

Despite being the host of TV's *Fun House* and having a ridiculous mullet hairstyle, Pat Sharp was a brilliant DJ. When I first walked into the studio to be introduced to him, I remember being a bit nervous. He actually looked really cool after shaving off his silly mullet, and also very young. Pat has a youthful face and still, to me, looks younger than I am. He became a good pal to me at the station straight away. In fact, Pat was the first DJ to make me feel really welcome. One day during my first week in the building, before I'd even presented my first show, he bowled into the tiny DJ office with his hand out towards me.

'Chris, welcome to Capital. You must be so excited.'

'Yeah, I am. I can't wait.'

'Neither can I. I've heard some good things about you and I'm really looking forward to hearing your first show.' I swear he was more excited than I was. I used to nick his headphones to wear during the show because they were the loudest pair. After Pat was – amazingly – fired from the station, I found the headphones in my pigeonhole with a note saying 'See you soon'. Bless him.

Other DJs and staff were cool to me. Neil Long was another DJ I really liked. And of course the gorgeous Margarita Taylor, who was very sexy, but slightly odd. She was beautiful, talented, earned some good money and still lived with her mum!

Sadly not all the DJs were as friendly.

A guy called Martin Collins presented the late-night show. He had a very smooth chilled-out voice to suit the late-night style. One night I followed him on the air presenting the overnight show. He seemed nice enough when I met him but didn't really say a lot to me. He left the studio and I started the show.

'Thanks to Martin Collins for the past few hours. He is such a laid-back guy, isn't he? I've never seen anybody that laid-back. I tell you, if he was any more relaxed he'd be in a coma.'

It was an old line but it worked well enough and I got on with the rest of the show. The next time I saw Martin, he blanked me. And it was a proper blank too. The time after that he blanked me again. What a rude fucker, I thought to myself. This carried on for a while until eventually I asked somebody about it.

'He's still pissed off at you for what you said on air about him.'

'Pissed off at me for saying what?' I asked.

'When you said on air that you wished he was in a coma. He thought that was really out of order.'

ARE YOU FUCKING KIDDING ME?

It turns out that after he left the studio that first night, he walked down the corridor and into the toilet. Somewhere between the corridor and the urinals he missed some of what I said. So what he actually heard was: 'Martin Collins … be in a coma.'

He never forgave me for the rest of my time there. Luckily I have seen him since and we shared a laugh over it. It's amazing what beer can do to bond a relationship!

Even though Martin blanked me for pretty much most of my time at Capital Radio, he wasn't the worst. That honour goes to somebody else entirely. Ladies and gentlemen, I give you the ego that is:

DOCTOR NEIL FOX.

Neil Fox was a proper deejay. He presented the evening show called 'The Surgery' so had the nickname to go with it. He wasn't a real doctor, by the way. Or, for what it's worth, a real fox! In fact, when he strutted round the office he reminded me of a pigeon. Foxy was very guarded with me and I heard that he was turned off by my style of presenting. He would make comments about me to the other DJs that weren't the most complimentary.

'Oh ignore him, he's just jealous,' I was told.

Jealous of what? I was earning £22K a year and drove a second-hand Renault Clio. He was on six figures and drove a classic Harley Davidson. I think it's fair to say, though, that I did admire him somewhat. He was, after all, a very well-known DJ who had achieved a lot. So I suppose I was disappointed when Doctor Neil Fox turned out to be a bit of an arsehole, to me anyway.

If I saw him in the studio and he was on his own, he would be fine with me. As soon as anybody else was in the room, he would change. He would take the piss out of me and try to belittle me in front of whoever it was. I was moved to a Sunday-night show and had to walk into his studio every single week.

'Here comes the shock jock,' he would say as I walked in.

'Hey hey, here comes Tubby,' was another introduction.

'Oh here he comes, desperate Dan.'

Desperate Fucking Dan? Go fuck yourself you fucking fuckhead.

I didn't actually say that back to him because I was a pussy and I found it intimidating. I just didn't know how to react to it. But later I got to slag him off repeatedly on my show on Radio 1. Petty, I know, but it was good fun and was my attempt at payback.

While I worked at Capital I rented a room from a guy I worked with called Ashley Tabor. Ashley was an assistant to Clive Dickens but he lived in a penthouse apartment on Baker Street.

'Jesus, how much money do you earn, pal?' I said as I walked in and saw the size of the place.

It turned out that Ashley's dad was, to put it mildly, fooking minted. Ashley and I got on very well and he was very funny. He had access to lots of money but was very down-to-earth about it. One day we went to Harrods to buy some televisions and videos for the apartment. He spent thousands that day. That was more money than my girlfriend at the time earned in a year.

'How can you justify spending that much money?' I asked him.

'Well, I know it's a lot, but I really want these televisions and I have the money, so why not?'

It made sense.

One day, after I'd been at Capital almost a year, I got a message to call a guy at BBC Radio Five Live. I had no idea what it was about so I got Ashley to call on my behalf, thinking that it made me look more important than I really was.

'So what do they want?' I asked him afterwards.

'It wasn't Five Live at all. It was Radio 1. They want to talk to you about a job.'

'WHAT?'

It turned out that a guy called Jeff Smith had been trying to contact me secretly without Capital finding out. He wanted to meet me and have a drink and a chat about my future plans.

LIVING IN LONDON

It's a Wednesday afternoon as I write on my keyboard at home in north London. I recently shifted the table from my conservatory (it was there when I bought the flat, it isn't posh and it leaks every time it rains) to the living room. Well, it's less of a living room, more of a room with a couch and a TV, a pile of DVDs and a kitchen strapped to the end of it. That's the thing about living in London. You live in a flat. Forget the house that you were brought up in, in London you live in a flat. I'm so used to it now that I only ever think about it when I talk to people who have never been to London and bought their house two streets away from Mum and Dad for £60,000. In London, you can't buy a house. Well, not unless Daddy buys it for you as a present. Or your great-grandma that you never met left it to you in her will. No, in London, unless you're super-rich, you live in a flat because:

YOU CAN'T AFFORD A HOUSE!

Seriously, I bought my flat in 1998. For the same money in Leeds I could buy a street. Moyles Avenue. Consisting of eight terraced houses and a shop that sells fruit, veg, chocolate bars and cigarettes. My mum said to me at the time: 'Is it worth it?'

Of course it isn't worth it! Not in Leeds terms anyway. However, in this strange place they call London, the flat next door will be the same price, so yeah, it's kind of worth it.

It's just another fact of living in London that you get used to. Here are a few facts about living here.

You don't know anybody who owns a house in London.

This is so true I can't tell you. I live in a flat. Comedy Dave lives in a flat. Rachel lives in a flat. Aled *shares* a flat. Dominic Byrne, my news-reading man, *does* live in a house – it's thirty miles out of London. The only person I know who owns a house near where I live is Chris Martin, the lead singer of the band Coldplay.

Which leads me to my second point:

If you do own a house – you're very rich.

Vernon Kaye owns a house. I rest my case.

Cab drivers either talk a lot – or simply grunt at you.

I used to live on Baker Street, which was a fifteen–twenty-minute walk to the Radio 1 studios. I'm not sure exactly how long it takes because back in those days I wasn't the fit, health-conscious walker that I am today. No, sir. Back then, I took cabs *everywhere*. I'd finish the early breakfast shift at seven o'clock, go for breakfast, then head out onto the street to flag down a cheery Cockney cab driver, only too happy to drop off a hard worker after his night shift.

BOLLOCKS! They were never happy. I used to *hate* getting a cab because the cabbies were always so miserable about driving you to where you wanted to go.

'Corner of Baker Street and Marylebone Street, please,' I'd happily say.

'Grunt,' would be the reply. If I was lucky.

Sometimes it would be a tut. Other times they would actually say *nothing*, just shrug the shoulders and look away. Now I appreciate it won't be the most money they'll earn all day, but it is a quick and easy job. It's not my fault it's not going to pay them £12.50. What do they want me to do?

MOVE FURTHER AWAY JUST TO PLEASE THE FUCKING CABBY?

It really does amaze me how miserable some of these cab drivers are. They genuinely get the arse for driving you somewhere that is only going to be a few quid. You never hear firemen moaning that it's only a small fire! Or a nurse in casualty bitching because a patient has accidentally cut their leg open as opposed to being stabbed in the middle of their forehead!

If they're not grunting at you, they're talking to you. Why am I interested in the roadworks in Peckham that are causing 'a cock arp wiv va traffic'?

I'M NOT!

'Do you know, that road down there has got six speed bumps on it.'

I DON'T CARE!

"Ere, I've just come back from Spain [it's always Spain] and I bought this chain out there for the equivalent of twenty pounds.'

Aaarrrghhhh!

SHUT UP. I'm not interested. I just want to make a phone call while you drive me to my destination, please. And that's another thing. That little bloody red light that goes on when they switch their intercom on. You tell them you're just going to make a phone call, so you switch it off. I've been in cabs when they SWITCH IT BACK ON AGAIN. I know, because that red light comes back on. I switch it off and it comes back on again. We end up playing a bizarre game of tennis intercom. JUST STOP IT. We all know you can hear through the glass anyway.

Now I do want to stress that not all cab drivers in London are like this. A lot of them are very friendly professionals who are doing a good job. In other words, don't talk to me about this when I jump in the back of your cab! Anyway, back to my facts about living in London.

The sewers have trains inside them.

It's an old Roy 'Chubby' Brown gag but it's true. It's called the Tube. A tiny, dirty train with little or no air-conditioning that is overcrowded and packed to the rafters with miserable, tired commuters who aren't allowed to look anybody in the eye. I believe that's an actual law. If you break the law and look at someone, they are allowed to beat you up or start a drunken conversation with you. You have been warned. I don't actually get the Tube, though, 'cos there's no first-class or butty wagon like on normal trains!

If your friend lives three miles away, it will take you one hour to get there. Half an hour if it's two in the morning.

Traffic in London is shite. Seriously, it's rubbish. I've seen traffic queuing up at 1.15 in the morning on the smallest roads. Car after car sitting there, polluting the air with their exhaust fumes. It takes so long to go the shortest routes in this bloody city. The Mayor of London a few years ago had a plan to solve this problem. Charge people to drive into the centre of London. Genius. I hate the congestion charge. It's a royal pain in the arse. Our studios are just inside the zone. So if I ever want to drive to work it will cost me another £8.00 for the privilege. Get a cab, I hear you say. Look at what you just read!

Nobody ever knocks on your door unexpectedly.

My mum grew up in Dublin. Not only did people just call round to say hello, but they wouldn't even knock and wait for someone to open the door. They knock as they open the door. It's a friendly place where you pop round to your friend's house and have a quick brew and a natter. Not in London. Again, I believe it to be some strange law that bans you from doing so. If Sophie and I are in and somebody knocks on the door, we look at each other blankly. Chances are it's a murderer or a drunk man or something. It wouldn't be a friend because friends always call before popping round. As I said, it's a strange place this London.

And here's possibly the worst thing.

You need a parking permit to park outside your own home.

I pay to park my car outside my flat. The local council give out more permits than there are spaces, so it doesn't necessarily mean I can actually park right outside the flat, or even on the same road. During the day most of the people who live on my street go to work. They decide to drive (foolishly) and the space where their cars sit all night long become empty. During the day it's never a problem for visitors to park in my street – so long as they have a visitor's parking permit. Hordes of traffic wardens roam the empty street looking for a car without the correctly scratched-off visitor's permit. The day, the month and the exact time you arrive need to be scratched off on the correct crappy permit. It may be half an hour or two hours. If you want to park for the day, that's a little more tricky. My local council grants me only ten all-day visitor permits a year! It's unbelievable. If a friend was in need of somewhere to stay, he could stay here, but only for ten days, after that his car would be clamped then towed away.

It's also the most difficult thing in the world to renew my parking permit. The friendly local council sent me a letter explaining that, according to their records, my car's permit will run out on this particular date and that I should renew it. They know what type of car I drive, the registration plate and the date the permit runs out. They also know where I live, as they have kindly posted me the letter with all of the above information. The letter tells me that if I want to renew my permit, I have to visit one of their tedious offices which is full of posters saying how great they are and that most customers are seen within ten minutes of arrival. It's never ten minutes, by the way. Oh, and please bring with you: proof of where you live, proof of what car you drive and proof of your driving licence. Insane. They write to me at my home, and then ask me to prove I live there. They tell me what my car is, and then ask me to prove that it's mine. Only in London!

PS. As I was writing this, it rained. The conservatory leaked again. Bastard thing.

14
FINALLY, I MAKE IT TO RADIO 1

was very happy working at Capital Radio in London. It was an amazing place to work and so exciting broadcasting to such a cool city. I was presenting a Sunday-night show and covering for the other DJs on the overnight shows so I was ready to move on to my own regular programme. Capital Radio were going through the process of buying Virgin Radio and Richard Park, the boss, dangled the carrot of a better slot in front of me. He called me into the office and explained what he wanted to do to change the sound.

'I have a challenge for you, if you're up for it,' said Richard.

'Sure. What is it?' I said, hoping it would be a better job than working in the middle of the bloody night.

'I'm going to move Doctor Fox to start later in the evening, and I'm thinking of putting you on Virgin to go up against him. Could you handle that challenge?'

Wait a second. He's offering me the late show on Virgin Radio, which is a national radio station, and I'd go up against Doctor Fox. And he's asking me if I can handle it? I looked Richard straight in the eye.

'Richard. You put me up against Foxy and I'll completely kill him in the ratings.'

Richard smiled back at me. 'That's exactly what I wanted to hear. And I bet you would too.'

This was a great chance for me to make an impact on national radio. The only problem was that it was ruled that Capital Radio would dominate too much of the London radio market if they bought Virgin and the deal was stopped. Shite. Luckily there were plans to move Martin Collins from the Capital FM late show, and I immediately set my sights on that. I talked to Richard and he said he would think about it. I knew I had to impress him a bit more.

Meanwhile I had received the call from Radio 1 and was intrigued to see what they wanted. I called Jeff Smith back; he was the head of music policy at Radio 1. We met up for a drink and a chat and got on well. He was a pleasant-looking short man with glasses, who reminded me of Penfold from the *Dangermouse* cartoons. He told me he liked what I was doing but wanted to hear me do a tape pretending to be on Radio 1. Now this was a problem. Richard Park knew *everything*. If there was a secret in the radio industry, he would know about it, and I knew that if I sneaked into Radio 1 to do a pilot show, he would find out about it.

'I'm on air every weekend. Why do you need me to make a tape? Just listen to it,' I said.

'Yeah, but it's not just me. There's the controller of the station, Matthew Bannister, and his number two Andy Parfitt to deal with as well. They have to hear you,' explained Jeff.

'Hang on. I appreciate they're busy but all they've got to do is switch the fucking radio on and listen to the show!'

Now granted I was being a bit mouthy but come on, it's radio, and it's one

Watching football in Portugal during Euro 2004

My 30th birthday at Radio One.
Party hats, balloons . . . but no bloody cake!

Mouldy Lookin' Stain.
Oh dear.

Fake publicity shot for our fake fitness video.

LANDS END 87

Some Beano thing.

Dressed as a dog at work.

Longman →

Chas (or Dave)

Dave (or Chas)

on my 32nd birthday

2005 - On top of the Empire State Building.

Me and Dave pose as crap NY cops. Tubby and Foil.

About to set off on the Red Nose rally.

JOHN O'GROATS 2005

LANDS END 874   PENTLAND SKERRIES 6

CHRIS MOXLES RED NOSE

ORKNEY & SHETLAND ISLES

The team with Sir Elton John.

ME WITH LOTS OF FAMOUS WOMEN ...
AND TAKE THAT!

Destiny's Child

Charlotte Church

Paris Hilton

The Queen.

Pink

Davina

Girls Aloud

Jordan

Madonna

ME WITH MEN

Robbie

50 Cent

WHYTE AND MACKAY

Kanye West

97-9

Sir Elton

Ozzy

P Diddy

Peter Kay

Chris Martin

Louis Walsh

Will Smith

Sophie Vernon George Clooney Kieron

Me and Boo at Disney

of the easiest mediums to connect to 'cos all you gotta do is find a radio and tune it in. I'd never worked at the BBC before. Maybe I had got it all wrong and all the bosses were fingerless suits like aliens from a *Doctor Who* episode. Or maybe I should just do the bloody tape!

Jeff and I chatted some more until we agreed that maybe making a tape wasn't best thing to do and Jeff said he would call me. At this time I had just taken on my first ever agent. I thought that when it came to dealing with the big boys at the BBC I would be out of my depth and that I could do with some help. I went to see the only agent who had shown any interest in me. His name was Tony Fox. My image of an agent back then was of a tall man in an overcoat smoking a big cigar and shouting loudly down his mobile phone about deals and money. Close. Tony wasn't the tallest man in the world. He did wear an overcoat, but it was more like the type Frank Butcher would've worn in *EastEnders*. He smoked cigars and spoke in a gruff London accent. He looked like a second-hand-fucking-car salesman. However, he was all that I had and I liked the guy, so why not?

I explained to Tony about the Radio 1 thing and asked him to speak to Richard Park at Capital and see if I could have the late show. Now I was buzzing. It was thrilling and nerve-racking at the same time. Oddly, as much I was impressed by Radio 1 approaching me, I really wanted the late show on Capital. Tony spoke to Richard, who again just said, 'We'll see.'

Jeff called and asked if I could meet up with him again, but this time Matthew Bannister the controller would be there. This was getting serious. I met them and we started talking. Matthew was well known in the industry. He had a great reputation from GLR, the BBC station for London, but he had changed Radio 1 so much when he arrived that the figures dropped, a lot, and it was barely clawing its way back. He was asking me to work at Radio 1, and I was honoured to be asked, but unbelievably, even though this was my dream,

I STARTED TALKING MYSELF OUT OF THE JOB!

I thought, back then in my young self, that I wasn't yet ready for national radio and needed another couple of years. I remember Matthew looking at me as if I was nuts. And why shouldn't he?

I WAS FUCKING NUTS!

There he was offering me the job of my dreams, and I was telling him that he was wrong and I wasn't ready!

'You *are* ready, Chris. I've heard the show and I think you'll fit right in with what we're trying to do with the station. I want to start you off on the early show, 4 a.m. until 7 a.m., leading up to the breakfast show, and then integrate you into the rest of the mainstream line-up,' said Matthew.

'I appreciate what you're saying but I'm out of the habit of working five days a week. I think it'll be better if I spend a few more years at Capital, and then I'll be ready.'

WHAT WAS I SAYING?

'Chris. Trust me, I know what I'm talking about. You have a very rare individual talent and I want you to come and work at Radio 1.'

JESUS, THE GUY'S ALMOST BEGGING ME.

'And I'm so flattered, Matthew, but I'm just not sure.'

NOT SURE ABOUT WHAT, YOU STUPID FAT IDIOT?

'Well, why not have a think about it, and let us know what you've decided.'

OH MY GOD, WHAT AM I DOING? TAKE THE JOB, CHRIS!

'OK, Matthew, thanks. And it was nice meeting you.'

And that was that. I'd been offered a job on BBC Radio 1, and I was going away to think about. What a dumb-arse.

I got Tony to call Richard Park and tell him the news. I knew that Richard would want to keep me and maybe even offer me more money than Radio 1 had, which was £50,000.

WRONG!

I was sitting in my flat in Milton Keynes when Tony called me and gave me the results of his conversation.

'Yeah, Chris, it's not good,' said Tony.

'What do you mean, it's not good? What did he say when you told him about Radio 1's offer?'

'Well, he said that he still hadn't thought any more about you doing the late show and if you wanted to go then you could go.'

I couldn't believe it.

'What about the money?' I asked.

'He said he'd offer you £40,000 to stay and not a penny more.'

This wasn't good. I was shocked that Richard wasn't prepared to fight for me. He hadn't even offered me the same money, let alone any more. I was deflated, but I was also very angry. As it turned out, it was to be the best thing anybody in radio had ever done for me.

'Right, Tony. Fuck Richard Park. Fuck Capital. Fuck the lot of them. Call Matthew and tell him I'll take the job at Radio 1.'

THE SONY RADIO AWARDS

The Sony Radio awards are the only officially recognised radio awards in the UK. I hate them. Seriously, I hate the awards. The night is full of DJs, probably the most annoying set of people on the planet, and ex-bosses of mine who forget they fired me and tell me how they always knew I'd make it. Piss off.

Each year, Radio 1 enters my show and has done so since 1997. We have never won the gold. It has become an annual event to talk about the awards on air. Every year we put in a tape of what we think is our funniest stuff. We wait for the list of nominations. Some years we don't get nominated. We never win those times. Other years we do get nominated, and we don't win those times either. Now I know it shouldn't bother us, but it does.

One time I asked on air for our listeners to tell us what they thought were the funniest bits of the year. The things we did that really made them laugh out loud. At that point we were doing the afternoon show and had about five million listeners, so we were going to get a fair sample of what was good. We went through thousands of text messages. On the list were interviews with famous people. Random links that ended up in fits of laughter. And the now legendary (on our show anyway) Eminem parody called 'Stanta', a Christmas version of his hit 'Stan', which we still play today. We make the tape, enter it and pay the entry fee (oh yes, you pay to enter) and sit back and wait to see if we have been nominated.

NOTHING.

We didn't even get a nomination. Five shows are nominated, of which there are three winners: bronze, silver and gold. We weren't even good enough, in the eyes of the judges, to get a colour that's duller than bronze! Not even a brown or a black award.

After a year on the breakfast show, we entered again. By now we all thought it was a pointless effort. And trust me: it is a huge effort. The work needed on these tapes is ridiculous. You have to go through a year of show notes, finding all the very best bits of the show. You also have to find one individual show that was funny from start to finish. Then there is the process of editing and copying the tapes. The application form needs to be filled in with comments and explanations of what the show is about and who works on it. The fee to enter is about £100. If you get nominated, you need to buy your places at a table and pay for food and drink. If you win, you receive one award. If you would like additional awards for Dave, or Rachel, you have to pay extra. This is one of the reasons why we don't look at it that we're not winning – we look at it that we are saving the BBC money.

Anyway, after twelve months of doing the breakfast show we had added an extra one million listeners. I had won several awards, including the Variety Club DJ of the Year, Loaded magazine's Lafta award, the Sun newspaper's DJ of the Year, GQ Man of the Year and even the Young Personality of the Year in the Yorkshire Young Achiever awards. A proud moment at Elland Road in

Leeds with Mum and Dad there to cheer me on. In case you haven't heard of these particular awards, they are a big thing in the Yorkshire area. They're sponsored by a firm of solicitors.

Anyway, our beloved leader at Radio 1, Mr Andy Parfitt, was convinced we would win something because of our huge success. The rest of us were not so sure. I hate being right all the time. We won nothing. At the time of writing this we have just been asked to enter again. Not one person on the show wants to do it. I bet we win this year.

There was, however, a moment in my radio career when we came very close indeed. Back in 1998 I was nominated for the DJ award. I hadn't even been on air at Radio 1 for twelve months and I was really excited about it. The awards were, and still are, held at the very nice Grosvenor House Hotel in London. In those days there were only three nominations per category, so you knew at least you would win the bronze. Jo Whiley had also been nominated. As much as I thought we wouldn't win, I knew we'd have a better chance than Jo. Now please don't take this the wrong way, but let's be honest:

I'M BETTER THAN SHE IS.

Since January 2004, our paths now cross every morning as she takes over from me at ten o'clock. I love Jo now. Not that I didn't then ... but I didn't. She was a bit cold towards me. Not horrible, just didn't make much of an effort. I was told that she was shy. Shy? She didn't say anything to me for the first four years, with the exception of a very timid 'Hi' every three months. Anyway, these days we get on very well. I really do like her and also think that one day she'll give in to my advances and charm and end up having me after a Christmas party.

So there we are at the awards in 1998. Sitting at the table is Jo and her producer Pat Connor. I'm sitting in an ill-fitting suit with my producer Ben

Cooper. Both Ben and I know that we don't really stand a chance, but then again there's the Jo factor. It gets to our award, and as the host (Joanna Lumley of all people) begins to read what the judges were looking for, Jo looks at me.

'It's going to be you,' she whispers.

'No, it'll be you,' I lie.

'No, it's gonna be you,' repeats Jo.

'No no, it'll be you,' I lie again.

We turn and look at the stage.

'And the winner of Best DJ 1998 is ... Jo Whiley!'

Oh bollocks.

Still, I was (fairly) pleased for her. Ben and I clapped and smiled. We knew we wouldn't win, and now that it was announced, at least you could just be pleased for Jo, whose face had dropped. I really believe she was more surprised than we were. Jo goes up to the stage and says her thank-yous. More people clap, then she heads back to our table. During all of this, Ben and I are trying to read the autocue to find out if we've won the silver or the bronze. Cue Joanna:

'Well done, Jo. The bronze goes to Ed Doolan (or someone) and the silver to Chris Morales.'

CHRIS MORALES?

Who the fuck is Chris Morales? That's not my name. It's Moyles. M O Y L E S. What the fuck is that all about? Not only do we lose to Jo Whiley, but now they're calling me Chris Morales. Bastards.

15

THE SHIT TIMES

It's not always been an easy ride. In fact, to be honest, most of it has been bloody bumpy. I've been fired. I've been out of work. Even after I'd got the job at Radio 1 there were people working there who hated my guts. I don't know why, 'cos I'm a nice guy. Really. If anything, I'm too nice. This is why I love doing the radio show every day. I can be more of the person I want to be because people think that *that* is the act.

For example, my girlfriend Sophie, whom I love very much and still think looks well fit, often wants me to go with her to visit some of her boring friends. I don't want to go, but I go anyway because we have one of those compromise relationships. It's only fair. I make her do tons of stuff she doesn't want to do. I mean, would you sit with me in the pub while Hirsty and I discuss our favourite radio jingles? Exactly. We compromise. Which means occasionally I have to go and be bored by some of her dull friends. They're not all dull, but you know what I mean. I bet you have exactly the same thing with your other half. And just to make sure she doesn't tell me off for writing that, I know there are some of my friends she finds dull. Or geeky. Or weird. Or creepy. Or very boring. Or, in one particular case, all of the above. I try to keep her away from that person as much as I can. Anyway, on our way home from seeing her dull mates, Sophie will tell me that she's proud of me for going and that I did well. It's here I have to point out that I don't do much. I don't go anywhere. I'm kind of like a hermit. I like my place and where I live and the pub round the corner. That's it. Why venture out? Hence Sophie will often tell me well done for actually leaving the house and talking to strangers. Then she'll ask me the dreaded question:

'You looked as if you enjoyed yourself. Did you?'

Aaarrrghhh.

What do I say? Do I tell her the truth?

Of course I didn't enjoy myself. I got stuck talking to some geek who wanted to tell me all about his recent skiing trip to somewhere in France I can't remember the name of. To top it all was the bloke who was so dull that neither you nor your friends would talk to him because you already know he's so MIND-NUMBINGLY BORING!

No, I don't say that. I tell her it was OK and that everybody was fine.

Then we go to sleep. I wake up at 5.20, get in the shower, get dressed, go to work, then tell all my listeners about the awful night I had with the most boring people on the planet. And everybody involved thinks I'm joking. It's all part of the act.

WELCOME TO MY LIVING HELL.

What is the truth and what is a lie? Sometimes even I don't know. The truth is that Sophie has some great friends. Paul is one of her best. He is very funny and looks like a mixed-up version of Ali Campbell from UB40 and Roy Kinnear, the dead actor. Then there's Vicky and Jamie. Jamie is a builder who has a permanent tan. He's like a good-looking version of David Dickinson. There are a few idiots in there but to be honest Sophie and I are so sickly together that we like the same people and we dislike the same people. Pretty much.

Anyway, I got off the subject. I am a nice person. I'm just a bit of a git on the radio. It's what I do. When I got to Radio 1 there was a woman who didn't see eye to eye with me.

One day I get called into her office because one of the other DJs has complained about something I said about them. I think it was Nicky Campbell but I'm not sure. I once made a joke about him being so thick that he visits prostitutes but only for the conversation. Anyway, I explain it was only a joke but she tells me that because I was new, maybe I shouldn't mention that DJ again.

Whatever.

A few weeks later, I'm called into the office again. Guess what? Another DJ has been moaning about comments I've made about them. This could've been anybody. It may have been Mark Goodyear – apparently as a joke, I said he had an ugly wife. In my defence, I can't remember saying that and I had never even met her so I had no idea what she looked like.

'Chris, this is my wife. You called her ugly on air once.'

Then he walked off and left me with her!

It all ended well. I explained it was a joke and she thought I was an arsehole.

Back in the office, I explain these things are only jokes, but once again I'm told not mention Mark on air any more.

Fine.

Then one morning I'm on air and Kevin Greening is in the studio next door. Kevin co-hosted the breakfast show at the time with Zoë Ball, who was always late. (If she was Father Christmas the kids wouldn't get anything until March.) Before he went live on air, Kevin had a habit of testing his microphone levels with the usual '1, 2, 1, 2, testing, oooonne, twoooo'. I would often have a little listen and I always found this very amusing. So one week I sneaked a tape into his studio and recorded a week's worth of '1, 2, 1, 2, testing, oooonne, twoooo'. I then mixed it down over the dance track 'Children' by Robert Miles and introduced it on air as the 'Kevin Greening 1-2 mic check mix'. He went absolutely ballistic. He didn't speak to me for about a month. Seriously, he just ignored me for weeks. His producer had a word with me and explained that Kevin felt I had taken the piss out of him. Then guess what? I get called into the woman's office again and told that a DJ had complained about me. This time, she is so fed up with me,

THAT SHE BANS ME FROM TALKING ABOUT ANY OTHER DJ ON AIR EVER AGAIN!

What the hell is that all about? How do I say who's coming on next, if I'm not allowed to mention their name? I tried to explain that maybe all the other DJs were super-emotional and that maybe they should all 'chill the fuck out'. This went down like a ton of bricks and I was told to leave her office.

I hadn't even been there for twelve months at this point.

Maybe this wasn't going to be as easy as I thought.

THE SONY AWARDS UPDATE

Well, would you Adam and indeed Eve it, as they say in that there London. I finally won a Sony Gold Radio Award. Hurray. The Sony Radio Awards 2006 were held last night at the Grosvenor House Hotel in London's trendy wherever-it-is. It was a bit weird because I haven't been for a few years so was a bit nervous about the whole thing. As well as that, Leeds United were playing in the second leg of the Championship play-off semi-finals against Preston.

If Leeds win this game it means we are heading to Cardiff to play either Watford or Crystal Palace in the finals, and whoever wins that game is promoted to the Premiership, which, just in case you don't know, is like the bestest of all the football groups in the whole wide world ever. This would be amazing for Leeds and would get the club back to where it belongs. Now, I don't have any problem with Crewe or Plymouth Argyle, but I'd rather see us play against Arsenal or Chelsea. So the pressure was on and I was feeling it. Plus the awards are held downstairs in the hotel in a massive ballroom so you can't get any signal on your phone to ring home and find out what the score is. Instead I had to sit through the ceremony, watching Radio East Ardsley win Local Radio Station of the Year, or trying my best to avoid wannabe DJs who tell me that they too started in hospital radio, like me. However, unlike me, they are still there. The more the night went on, the more anxious I got about our little game of football.

At half-time at the awards ceremony, I managed to make my way upstairs so I could call my parents, who were watching the game at home. (I recently bought my mum and dad Sky+ Television as a Christmas present. Normally my dad wouldn't be interested in such fangle-dangle satellite-dish things. He's your typical down-to-earth, normal, hard-working, stubborn, northern working-class lad who's not bothered by technology. However, on a recent phone call to my mum back home, I was informed that she was now relegated to the back room on certain evenings. The reason for this was that Mr Not-bothered-by-Sky would plonk himself on the couch and tuck into Sky Sports, or Sky Sports2, or Sky Sports Evening News or anything with the word Sport in it. Bless them. Finally a present my dad actually likes!)

Anyway, I call them and Mum and Dad are indeed watching the game. It was 0–0 at an extended half-time after a problem with the floodlights; both teams were just running onto the pitch for the second half.

Not too bad, I thought. We could win this if we scored first.

I made my way back downstairs to the countless dinner tables of the awards ceremony. I didn't have the dinner myself but heard that it was quite nice. How could I eat? I was missing an important match. Oh, and I was nominated for an award up against Jonathan Ross, Chris Evans and Danny

Baker. Suddenly, from another table, my executive producer Rhys leans over and whispers, 'It's one–nil to us, apparently.'

YEAH. GET IN, YOU SUPER LEEDS.

Then to the stage:

'And the winner is ... Scott Mills.'

YEAH. GET IN THERE, SCOTT MILLS.

Scott wins a gold award and Leeds are currently winning by a goal. Turning out to be an OK kind of a night.

'And the winner is ... Zane Lowe.'

YEAH. ANOTHER AWARD FOR ZANE.

He was nominated for two awards that night. Personally I think it's greedy and shows a self-righteous enjoyment of award ceremonies, which everybody else hates because they don't win.

Then my friend Jody sneaked up to me. 'It's two–nil to Leeds.'

YEAH. COME ON, SUPER LEEDS. YOU CAN DO IT.

'And the winner is ... Zane Lowe.'

AGAIN? THE GREEDY BASTARD!

I haven't won *one* gold award, and this guy, who incidentally pretty much wins at least two awards every bastard year, goes and picks up two *golds* in the one night. If he wasn't such a nice person, I'd—

'It's finished, Chris. Leeds win two–nil. We're going to Cardiff,' says a voice in my ear.

YES YES YES. WE DID IT!

'And the gold in the Entertainment Award goes to … Chris Moyles.'

AAARRRGGGGGHHHHH! WHAT A NIGHT.

What an absolutely brilliant night. I really didn't think I had a chance of winning so I hadn't bothered preparing anything. The only thing I had thought of doing was a big rant about how much these awards irritate me because of how unfair and wrong a lot of their choices are.

Thank you for this award. It's just a shame that it comes a little too late for me, at a time when it actually doesn't mean anything any more because the last few years the judges seem to have handed awards out to just about anybody who enters the competition, with of course the exception of me, and I consider it to be a huge waste of money to all these radio stations that enter and the talent they employ. I for one am not going to take it any more and would first like to hand the award straight back to these so-called judges who probably have never been on the radio in their lives, and invite anybody else who agrees with me to stand up now in a Jerry Maguire style and walk with me to the nearest pub where I will buy you a pint as we drink to the demise of these so-called Sony Radio Awards.

Or I could just say, *Thank you.*

I ran both these options past the boss of Radio 1, Andy Parfitt. He liked the second option better, saying that it was more gracious. Gracious? I've added a million new listeners to the breakfast show on Radio 1 and been ignored by these awards people and I'm meant to be gracious. Fuck 'em. Besides, as we were having this conversation some other winner came up and just said 'Thank you', so that was my great gag speech ruined. When I did win I hugged Andy and my team and brought them on stage with me. Well, Dave,

Rachel and Aled anyway. I wasn't going to bring *everybody* from the show up there. I always think that looks rubbish. Like this is the best thing ever to happen to them. Get a life.

I grabbed the microphone and said, 'About fucking time,' as I had waited sixteen years to get one of these awards. I was quite surprised that it got a decent laugh. Anyway, I said a few more things and then sat down. Then Radio 1 won the Radio Station of the Year award, which it has *never* won before. And Leeds United won too. And Scott Mills. And Zane Lowe (the greedy bastard!) and, of course, me.

As I've always said, I love the Sony Radio Awards people. They've got great taste.

16

X FACTOR
– OH JESUS!

How did I get myself into this ridiculous situation? I pondered this question several times in the space of about five minutes. The first time was when Paul Daniels walked over to me and said hello. Then when I accidentally mistook Dr Gillian McKeith for an old midget lady. The final time was while I was sat in a room with the dwarf lady, the old magic man, a woman who slept with the England football captain, some famous chefs and a page-three model with a northern accent. How did I get to be standing in a canteen surrounded by an extremely random selection of British celebrities?

BLOODY X FACTOR, THAT'S HOW.

I get asked to do a lot of silly television shows and I pretty much always say no. I say no for various reasons. Sometimes I don't like the show, or sometimes I love the show but don't want to go on it in case everybody I enjoy watching on it turns out to be a complete arsehole. It's now a habit for me to say no to most offers that arrive at my agent's office. Sophie is constantly moaning that I should do more stuff. I think there are two reasons why she does this.

> *It would be good for me to do it.*

> *She likes to go and meet the people involved and have a top night out.*

So when the offer came in to sing on *Celebrity X Factor*, or *X Factor, Battle of the Stars*, as it was – Sophie could barely contain her excitement.

'You've GOT to do it,' she screamed, as she bounced off one wall and onto the other. It was at this point that something odd happened to me. I didn't say no immediately. I actually thought about doing it and came up with reasons why I should. While Sophie was hurtling from one wall to the other, I came up with five reasons why I should do *Celebrity X Factor*.

I have a radio show to promote.

Even though the radio show has a very sizeable audience, it could always do with more listeners. I had no idea how many people would watch the TV show, but if it was nine million people and 10 per cent of the viewers decided to give my show a try, well, that's best part of another million listeners.

I have a book to promote.

Not only that, but I've got a book to bloody write. As I type this it is the day before the TV show starts. I am being picked up from my house in one hour at 11.20 a.m. on an average-looking Sunday morning. In five hours' time I find out which of the three now famous judges will be mentoring my category. This TV show might shift a few more copies of the book, and, more importantly, give me another thing to write about. Don't forget I'm a DJ, I ain't no J.K. Rowling! (No shit!)

I would like to learn how to sing.

Over the years I've recorded various parody songs on the radio. I love writing and singing them. It's a nice process to go from an idea about a song to writing it and then recording the vocals and mixing it all down. (I've made this process sound way too glamorous – I usually just sing different lyrics over the instrumental of the track.) I'm a good mimic. I can copy other people's voices – but I don't really know how to sing as myself. Now it may not be the coolest thing to admit, but fuck it, I think it would be interesting to learn to sing properly.

It'll pay for a holiday.

I *never* do a job just for the money. I've always believed that if I'm good at what I do, the money will naturally follow. I've thought this ever since I started when I was sixteen. However, in this job it's often difficult to turn something down because if they really *really* want you, they can throw a lot of money your way. *NOT X FACTOR, THOUGH!* The money by most standards is good, but I've got to take into account that if it doesn't work I'm going to look like a prize prick for the next six months, and in this business that has a price! However, if it goes to plan, it's a bit of money that will pay for a very nice holiday, and who wouldn't sing on the TV for a ten-day trip to Dubai?

Finally:

It'll be a good laugh.

Look, I'm living a bit of a dream here. One day this might all be over. I might have to get a proper job. Fifty thousand people audition to be on the real *X Factor* TV show, and I'm getting paid to do it. I watch the bloody thing at home every Saturday anyway, so to do it and get paid for it – it's a no-brainer. Plus, I might get a snog from Sharon Osbourne.

So that was that. Five reasons why I decided to stand on stage every night for a week on national television in front of an audience of millions. I thought that would be the easy part. The hard part was sitting in a room with the other 'celebrities' trying not to look like I'm taking it too seriously.

I thought I'd worked out how to play *X Factor*, how to deal with the judges Simon Cowell, Sharon Osbourne and Louis Walsh. Simon and Louis had been studio guests before on the radio show so I knew they'd be OK, and I'd met Sharon once or twice and knew that we'd get on well. Kelly Osbourne had been a studio guest a few times and we also got on well, so I knew that would help. Kate Thornton, the host, I'd met a few times before, too. I wasn't a massive fan of hers before the series. I had always assumed, as I often do, that she wouldn't really be interested in somebody like me on any scale. As it turned out, she was absolutely lovely to me. Virtually every night after my performance she would stand next to me effortlessly reading out the voting phone and text numbers as I pinched her arse out of camera shot. I liked her a lot, and she was brilliant at presenting the show as well.

So as far as the regular *X Factor* team went, I felt confident. All I had to do now was befriend the other 'celebrity' contestants. Or avoid them. And what a list of A-list stars it was. First was the legendary double act of:

PAUL DANIELS AND DEBBIE McGEE

Paul Daniels had been entertaining television audiences for years by the time I started watching TV. His 'glamorous' assistant, Debbie, was his wife, who would utter the then famous phrase 'Yes, Paul' every time she assisted him with a trick. Dominic our news guy had called him up once to ask whether he'd be interested in a TV show we had an idea for. It was called *Celebrity Hide and Seek* and we had talked about it on the radio show for a while. At the start of the conversation, Dom asked Paul how he was.

'I make a living,' was the reply. For some reason Dom and I found this an odd yet funny thing to say, and would often use it on the show if we ever spoke about the magic man. On the Sunday before *X Factor* started, we had to assemble at Fountain Studios in Wembley to meet each other and find out which judge would be our team mentor. There were nine acts, each with one mentor, in three teams: an under-twenty-five category, an over-twenty-five category and the groups. Paul Daniels was the first person to come up and say hello.

'Mr Moyles, I presume,' said the magic man.

'Hello, Paul, lovely to meet you. How are you?' I asked.

'I make a living!' was the reply.

I had to work out whether or not this was a box-standard line he uses a lot, or whether he'd heard us take the piss out of him and was trying to have a dig. I didn't have to wait long for the answer as I heard him use the same line another four times as he met the other contestants. On the first day he was quite annoying. Always chipping in with so-called funny lines or moaning about the amount of work we had to do and the money we were getting paid for it. I let him off with it because he's an old-fashioned entertainer. He was a TV legend, in the days when a star was a star with millions of viewers. His wife Debbie seemed nice. After spending time with both of them, I warmed to them a lot. The problem is this ever-changing fickle celebrity world we live in. These guys have seen it all before. They were *huge* television stars who commanded *huge* fees. Who were we to them? Nothing really. Once Paul had calmed down a bit from his silly one-liners, he was a sweet bloke. I managed to get him to show us a few card tricks, which were brilliant, it has to be said. So, Paul Daniels and Debbie McGee were nice. Debbie even took my number on the last day. So far she hasn't called me.

Next on the list was the glamour model:

MICHELLE MARSH

Michelle was the lesser-known half of a modelling duo with a girl called Lucy Pinder. I'd seen Lucy before at a soccer six-charity football event. I wasn't massively impressed. In the magazines she looks cute and sexy with a great body, but running round a pitch in a football strip with very little make-up on, she wasn't all that. So naturally I knew that Michelle and I would get on like Stevie Wonder in an eye test. Once again I was wrong. She was wicked. Very naturally pretty with an amazing body. She had a great figure and wore a dress on the first night that showed it off a treat. I know that sounds sexist, but I am talking about a woman who gets paid to get her tits out for the cameras, so she'll probably like the fact that I'm saying she looks nice with clothes on. She also had a great singing voice and was charming with it. She had a nice northern accent, which always works for me, had amazing eyes and seemed very down-to-earth.

On the last night of the show I found out that she had very ticklish legs. Her boyfriend really is a lucky man. But then again, is he? I mean, at least with Sophie men aren't always staring at her tits when they talk to her. They normally can't take their eyes off mine! When Michelle was voted off the competition she was really gutted. It was a shame for me too because she looked better in a dress than Paul Daniels.

Next on the list was:

NIKKI SANDERSON

Nikki had just left the TV show *Coronation Street*. I'd seen pictures of her in the papers and she'd always looked cute. Trust me, those pictures didn't do her justice. She was absolutely fooking gorgeous. She and Michelle were alike (and got on very well together), but Nikki was funnier. Sadly, though, Nikki wasn't as top-heavy as Michelle, but you can't have everything, can you? By the time the series had finished I had a huge soft spot for her. She was tiny and cute, had a great singing voice and was a real laugh. I met her boyfriend a few times during the show. Loud, brash and with a cockney accent thrown in, a complete opposite. As opposed to me, of course. An older, overweight, egomaniac with a confidence problem and a penchant for younger northern ex-soap actresses. Oh yeah, she didn't know what she was missing! Again on the last day we swapped numbers. She hasn't called either.

Back to group category, and please welcome:

REBECCA LOOS AND JAMES HEWITT

Now this was a combination made in television hell. A former army major who was dubbed as a love rat after an affair with Princess Diana, and a former personal assistant to David Beckham who allegedly slept with him, sold her story to the newspaper and did a big TV interview about it, before going on Channel 5 and pleasuring a pig. Oh what a line-up of stars we had. Now I know what most people reading this think of Rebecca Loos, and I probably agree with you. She became famous after sleeping with an England icon and spilling her guts about the whole thing to the world's press. I wasn't a fan. She seemed desperate for any kind of attention and it looked like she'd do almost anything to get on television or in the papers. But I'm a man with the thoughts and the brains of a man so I also had an extra view of her, which was the fact that she did have:

AN ABSOLUTELY PERFECT BODY.

Now I know that makes me shallow but I can't help it. I'm a man and all men are stupid. As it turned out, though, her nipples pointed in different directions. Not that dissimilar to my feet, which walk in a 'ten to two' action. She didn't talk to me that much, and when she did I got the impression that she had no idea who I was and no intention of finding out.

James Hewitt, on the other hand, was hilarious. His posh voice made me smile every time he spoke, and me and a few of the others were always getting him to say 'Ding Dong'. On the afternoon before the first show, myself, James and fellow contestant Matt Stevens were sharing a dressing room. We had finished rehearsal for the programme and had about an hour and a half to kill before the live transmission. I said I quite fancied a drink. At which point James placed his hand inside his suit jacket and pulled out the biggest hip flask I have ever seen. Matt and I were very impressed.

'Here, have a little of this,' said James in his exquisite voice.

'What's in it, James – whisky?' asked Matt.

'Oh no, don't be silly. It's sherry!' replied the posh major.

My girlfriend Sophie wanted to meet him after the first night, only so she could get him to say 'Ding Dong' to her. I saw him in the bar so we walked over and I introduced Sophie.

'This is my girlfriend Sophie,' I said.

'DING DONG,' he replied.

Sophie's face lit up like a Christmas tree. On the last night Sophie and I were walking through the corridors of the studios when James appeared walking down the stairs.

'Hey, James,' I said. 'You remember Sophie, my girlfriend?'

He took one quick look at her and immediately said: 'Ding and indeed Dong!'

Sophie almost wet herself laughing. He was funny and I liked him a lot. James and I swapped numbers after the show and so far I have received a couple of phone calls from him. One of the calls I received at 6.30 in the morning. He sounded like he'd finished the hip flask.

MATT STEVENS

I was told there would be a professional rugby player taking part in *X Factor*, and as my knowledge of rugby is approximately zero, I knew I wouldn't have any idea who it was, and I didn't. However, as soon as I met Matt, we got on. It was just as well because I met him on the Sunday before the series started, the day when all the contestants, or celebrities as we were called, met for the first time. By the time I'd met Paul Daniels and Debbie McGee, Rebecca Loos and Dr Gillian McKeith (more on her later), I was desperate to find somebody fairly normal.

Matt came over to me and introduced himself, saying that he was a big fan of the show. I must admit this always helps. Not just because it's flattering, which it is, but also because I'm not very good at meeting new people. As I said, I'm quite shy. I know a lot of people don't believe me, but it's true. I'm not a great mingle person and I'm not very confident at starting a conversation, so I don't normally bother. This results in people thinking I'm a rude bastard, which I'm not. Well, I can be, but never in these situations. I just don't really know what to say to people I've just met. So Matt making the first move was the best thing.

Once I was relaxed with him I could be myself, and as the days went by at the TV studios we ended up sharing a dressing room. Even when we had our own separate rooms, Matt would still insist on sharing with me. That was fine, in fact quite sweet, but he would arrive at about nine in the morning, and because I was still doing the radio show, I would roll in about two o'clock in the afternoon, by which time he would have managed to place his shit all over the dressing room. He was such a scruffy bastard, and don't even get me started about what happened when he went to the toilet in our shared cubicle. OH MY GOD! I accept that he's a big guy, after all he does play professional rugby for a living, but Jesus Christ, it was like he'd just eaten a dead dog and shat that out. (I promised Matt that I wouldn't tell that story in the book ... I lied!)

Matt's parents came over to see him from South Africa and they were very sweet. His dad is a massive man mountain as well. Incidentally, I do find it odd that he plays for England despite having South African parents and having been born in South Africa. I think he had a great-great-grandmother who once visited Liverpool and apparently that will do. Matt was a top fella and everybody thought it was going to be him and me in the final. As it turned out, I got knocked out on the penultimate night and he and Lucy Benjamin went through instead. Who saw that one coming? I didn't, and neither did Matt. Anyway we've promised to keep in touch and maybe I'll pop along and watch him play rugby. Then again I might just meet him after the game for a few beers instead.

THE CHEFS

Now *X Factor, Battle of the Stars* ran the same way in which the original TV show worked. The three judges each mentored their own category. Sharon Osbourne had the sixteen-to-twenty-four-year-olds Nikki, Matt and Michelle. Louis Walsh had the horribly titled twenty-five-and-overs category, comprising Lucy Benjamin, Dr Gillian McKeith and myself. And finally Simon Cowell looked after the group of Paul Daniels and Debbie McGee, Rebecca and James, as well as a very odd combination of four fairly well-known chefs. They were Aldo Zilli, an Italian restaurateur who owned a couple of places in London, whom I had met before. Jean-Christophe Novelli, JC as he was known, a French restaurateur and chef who made a name for himself doing *Hell's Kitchen* on ITV. Paul Rankin, a Belfast boy whose restaurant got the first ever Michelin star in Northern Ireland. And Ross Burden, a TV chef.

If you saw the show you will know they were absolutely terrible. They couldn't sing. They couldn't dance in time, and as for JC he couldn't remember the words or even pronounce them in a language that sounded anything like English. But they were bloody funny. When JC danced, he would wave his hands and legs round like a demented fly on a candle flame. I think he liked me too 'cos he kept referring to me as 'the funny man' and giving me hugs and kisses. Well, he is French. Sadly, though, I could never understand a bloody word he said. Ross blurted each line out with such a camp voice that he looked like somebody from a *Carry On* movie. Paul wasn't too bad, apart from being nervous every night and having to stare at the autocue 'cos he couldn't remember the words.

The best one was Aldo Zilli, who seemed to really want to be a singer. He took it so seriously. One night he forgot the words to his song and burst into the dressing room afterwards pissed off at himself. It was hilarious. Aldo and I would joke that even though we only signed up to do it for a laugh, when we stood backstage ready to go on, all of a sudden it became so serious that we forgot for a few minutes it was only a bit of fun. They lasted a lot longer than everybody thought, too – outlasting Michelle and Nikki. Who knows what the British public will vote for these days!

DR GILLIAN McKEITH

Before I went to the studios that first day to meet all the other 'singers', I'd expected a few egos to be flying around. I just wasn't sure which they would be. Who'd have guessed it would be the doctor!

All I knew about her was that she was some kind of nutritionist and she had her own show on Channel 4. I had heard that she was 'the Shit Woman', going through people's shit and telling them what they should and shouldn't be eating. Now that I just don't get. I'm no nutritionist myself, but even I know the rules of a good balanced diet.

Burgers and chips = Bad food

Fruit and vegetables = Good food

Done. I don't need to rummage through your poo to tell you that. That's just wrong on so many levels. (Every time I looked at her I wondered if she spent longer than the rest of us washing her hands. And if she didn't, she bloody well should.) I was apprehensive about meeting her as I'd said a few things on the radio about her that weren't exactly the nicest. Mind you, one of the woman's claims to fame is that she helped Michelle McManus lose loads of weight. Are you kidding me? How can that be something to shout about?

THE WOMAN'S STILL FUCKING FAT, FOR CHRIST'S SAKE!

Now don't get me wrong, the girl's done good to shift a lot of beef, and credit where credit's due, but do me a favour. I could help Michelle lose weight. I'd either staple her lips together or chop both her legs off.

Anyway, back to Dr Who, as some people nicknamed her. She's a very tiny woman who presents a show called *You Are What You Eat*. Taking that into account, she must have been eating some small prima donnas. During the first few days, she was late for things. Demanded extra time with the vocal coaches. Moaned about the sound, or the amount of time we had to rehearse. Everything seemed to be a problem. She actually started behaving like a real singer. Which she isn't.

SHE GOES THROUGH OTHER PEOPLE'S SHIT FOR A LIVING!

She also wasn't very good with her Ps and Qs. One afternoon we were standing at the top of the stairs waiting to go on stage. One of the floor managers, whose job it is to make sure we are where we are meant to be and don't miss our entrance, was standing with us.

'And can you make sure there's water here for tonight's show,' she demanded.

That pissed me off. 'Oi. Say please,' said me, being all high and mighty.

'What, are you my mother now, are you?' she replied, looking a bit shocked.

'No, I'm not. If you want water, ask nicely and say please.'

'I *did* say please.' She was getting a bit narked.

'No, you didn't. And it's not even his job to get you water. If you want some, ask nicely and be polite.'

Look at me. Chris Moyles, king of manners.

Strangely we got on better after that. Mind you, that could be because she got voted off that night and I didn't have to see her again until the final.

Incidentally, during the last few days of the run after she was voted off, Gillian called the production staff on the show and asked for the phone numbers of some of the other contestants so she could keep in touch. She never asked for mine.

LUCY BENJAMIN

Lucy is an actress who most famously played the part of Lisa Fowler in *EastEnders*. (I think she was a Fowler, but who cares, you know who she is.) I'd met Lucy once before, at a birthday party for Perry Fenwick, who

plays Billy Mitchell. Come to think of it, it was also the first time I'd met
Perry. I'd become pals with Michael Greco who played Beppe, and he and
Perry were good pals so I was invited to pop along to a north London pub
to have a few pints. Lucy Benjamin was also there, and looked like she
was enjoying herself. When I met Lucy at *X Factor* she seemed very keen
to say hello.

'Hey, I love your show. I've been dying to meet you,' she said.

'We've actually met before, Lucy – at Perry's birthday party.'

She looked at me with a slightly embarrassed but very confused look on
her face.

'Oh God, I don't remember that at all. I think I'd had a bit to drink.'

I *loved* Lucy straight away. She is instantly likeable, funny and charming,
honest and friendly. But she's also very bitchy in a very likeable way.
Needless to say, we got on like a house on fire. You know, if she wasn't
happily married and pregnant, I reckon I'd have had a chance there.

We spent a lot of our time at *X Factor* bitching about Dr Gillian behind her
back, or laughing and joking at the fact that we were doing *X Factor* and
singing on national television. As we had to rehearse the beginning of the
TV show *every single day*, Lucy and I spent a fair bit of time together.
At the start of every show we had to walk on together and stand there like
lemons, waving at the crowd. Now I'm taller than Lucy, and it's fair to say
that she has quite large breasts. Plus every night she wore an outfit that
showed them off very well. Standing there every night on national
television next to Lucy, I must admit I did glance down and look. I'm sorry,
I couldn't help myself. Plus Gillian McKeith was on the other side of me –
so where the hell would you look!

Lucy had some sweet habits. Each day when she saw me she would greet me with: 'Hello, sweetheart.' And give me a big cuddle. However, she had one habit that I know she won't like me telling, but it's the truth and it's also very funny. Each night just before the show went live on TV, Lucy and I would be sitting on the stairs at the right-hand side of the stage, ready to go on. It was at this precise moment that Lucy's nerves would kick in. Now, people react to nervousness in different ways. Some people sweat, others get short of breath. Lucy was different. Lucy ... would fart. Seriously, she would sit on the top step while I chatted with her from the bottom of the steps. All of a sudden she would say: 'I wouldn't come up here for a few seconds if I were you,' and let out a little bit of air!

Now maybe it was some woman pregnancy thing, but this happened *every night*. I've never known a woman trump so much. For the record, though, and I'm not just saying this because I like her, they didn't make a sound and they also smelt of rose petals!

Lucy started off the competition singing like a bag of scared kittens. By the end of the week, she had grown in confidence and her singing had got better and better. She ended up winning the whole damn thing. She was so pleased when she'd won. I stood at the side of the stage cheering her on. And even though I didn't see it, or hear it ... I'm sure she probably let out another one in her excitement!

So there you have it. My *X Factor* fellow 'celebrities'. I actually loved doing it. Most of us got on really well, and the crew behind the scenes were great too. I got on well with the judges, and Simon Cowell even agreed to write the foreword for this book. How cool is that? Although I'd have preferred him to buy me an expensive sports car. I mean, he can afford it, right? People told me after the show that I came across as a 'really nice guy' and how surprised they were. What a bloody cheek! I've always thought I was a nice guy anyway, but I suppose it's good to find out that people who thought I was an idiot have changed their view of me since. Plus, I also improved my singing, and got some nice clothes out of it too! Oh yes, God bless ITV and their stylists. A few suits, some nice shoes, some singing lessons, a magic trick from Paul Daniels and some fit women to hang out with for a week. And I got paid for it too. I really am a lucky bastard!

SIMON COWELL

I've always liked Simon Cowell. On television I find him watchable, and actually very likeable. I even read his book, which tells the story of his amazing life. How he had huge chart success with such acts as Robson and Jerome, Zig and Zag and the WWF wrestling superstars. It's funny how Simon is always referred to as Mr Nasty, or the rude one, when all he is is refreshingly honest and says exactly what you're thinking when watching the programme.

The only downside of doing *X Factor* was that Simon and I never got to have a go at each other. As I said, I like him, but I was well up for some TV banter. The only gag I got to do was on the last show. As I was voted out on the penultimate show – a fact I'm still finding hard to believe; after all, I did seem more popular than the ex-*EastEnders* actress and the rugby player with no neck put together, but still, that's the way it was – I had to come back on the last show and sing again with all the losers. This I did not want to do. Even seconds after I had been cruelly voted off, as they played my 'Best of' moments to the viewing public, I turned to

Louis Walsh and begged him: 'Jesus, please don't make me sing with all the other losers.'

He just smiled. The song was a medley of 'I'd Like To Teach The World To Sing' and Abba's 'Thank You For The Music'. I wanted to die. At rehearsal, we practised a couple of times and I felt my entire career slipping away from me. As I walked out singing, 'And hear them echo through the hills, ah peace throughout the land', before standing between Dr Gillian McKeith and Rebecca Loos, I swear that I could hear the faint voice of panto calling me. I was so uncomfortable with the whole routine that I spoke to one of the bosses to explain that I couldn't do it as it stood, and was there *anything* I could do to feel happier with it. After a while, we compromised: I would walk out wearing a mask. We got a guy to sneakily make a mask with two holes for the eyes so I could see, and then just before I walked out on stage, I pulled my trousers as far up my stomach as I could. Then it was my cue. I walked on the stage with my Simon Cowell face-mask and my trousers just above my man boobs and delivered my line. Then I mimed for the rest of the song! I could see Simon's face as he sat there watching and no doubt thinking to himself, 'What a little bastard.' But he liked it, which was lucky.

Behind the scenes, Simon thanked me for doing the show and we chatted about a couple of things, including the idea of me, *maybe*, recording a song. Louis Walsh was convinced, and still is, that I would have a number one record with 'What A Wonderful World'. I, however, am not so sure. The only thing left was to convince Simon I would work very well in America and that he should give me a TV show to do. I'm still waiting for that one. I could, however, use some blackmail. During the week of *X Factor*, Simon was planning a trip to the newest Stringfellows nightclub. He asked me if I fancied going. Of course I would, but Sophie has banned me from all such places and I'd rather upset Simon Cowell than Sophie any day of the week. As it turned out, while Simon was enjoying the surroundings of the club, he bumped into Zoë Ball. To cut a long story short, Zoë wanted me to win and therefore proceeded to dance for Simon as a kind of bribe so that I would win *X Factor*. As you know, I didn't. Which means Zoë is not cut out for a career in lap-dancing.

Anyway, Simon Cowell, I thank you. Oh, and don't forget my Ferrari. Cheers.

MY PARENTS

I know everybody says that they have the best parents in the world. Well, maybe not everybody. I don't think Macaulay Culkin does, or maybe even Michael Jackson, but I know I have the best parents in the world. First of all, they're still together. Even in the unlikely event of my dad actually wanting a divorce, I don't think my mum would let him.

My mum, Vera, was born in Dublin in Ireland, and my dad, Chris, was born and bred in Leeds in West Yorkshire but his family were from County Mayo in Ireland. He has this weird connection with the place and feels he belongs there. I don't know why. He dragged us all there once and it really is in the middle of bloody nowhere. It's the kind of place where the local pub doubles as the post office, police station and grocery store. Dublin, however, is a different story. A busy bustling city with lots going on, and of course plenty of pubs! Mum comes from a typically large Irish family consisting of six girls and only one boy, poor bloke. My uncle Michael has spent his entire life with six crazy, gossiping Irish sisters. I don't know how he hasn't emigrated to Australia.

Every single school holiday of mine was spent on a tiny prop plane from Leeds Bradford airport or on a bloody overnight ferry to Dublin. I was sixteen before I went anywhere else on holiday. It was Dublin all the bloody time, and it was not classed as going on holiday, it was 'going home'. Maybe to my mum it was going home, but not to me. Don't get me wrong, I love my Irish family, but a little trip to Spain would've been nice. Jesus, I would have even taken a weekend in France. We'd land in Dublin and be picked up by either one of my uncles or one of my cousins who could drive. Then it was straight to one of the family's houses. We *never* stayed in a hotel *ever*.

'Why would we stay in a hotel?' Mum would say.

'Oh I don't know, Mum, maybe because then there isn't nine of us sleeping in a three-bedroom house!' would have been my reply.

I'd walk through the door of the Irish family house and be greeted with: 'Look who it is, oh Jesus, welcome home. When are you going back?'

This happened every time. My dad always joked that it was the first thing anybody said to us: 'When are you going back?'

'We've only just bloody arrived,' he would answer.

Another odd thing was how they greeted me. Now granted, my aunties and uncles probably hadn't seen me for six months, but it was hardly like me walking through the door in the Secret Garden.

'Jesus, Christopher, you've grown.'

'Jesus, Christopher, you're putting on some weight, aren't ya!'

'Jesus, Christopher, you're a turning into a handsome lad now.'

After a while I started to believe that my name was 'Jesus Christopher'.

My dad's family was a lot quieter than Mum's. His mum and dad were my local grandparents in Leeds. His mum was a fairly typical granny. She had big white hair and looked a bit like the granny in *Postman Pat*. His dad, however, to me was like a one-man fairground. He had one and a half legs. He'd lost one of them from the knee down because of the war or something and had a plastic one fitted. In his plastic leg was a small hole which, Grandad told me, was caused by mice eating it. I believed this for years. Then when I was a bit older, Grandad lost his other leg and had to use a wheelchair. He was a very jolly man who liked to make jokes about being legless. But sometimes you would see him get a little agitated.

'What's wrong, Grandad?' I would ask.

'My foot's itching.'

'But, Grandad, you don't have any feet.'

'I know, son, that's why I don't know where to scratch.'

My dad has a similar sense of humour to his dad, and I suppose it's been passed down to me too.

Both my parents have always been incredibly supportive of my radio career. Even before it was a career they not only humoured me into thinking that I would make it one day, but they helped me financially and physically too. Those trips to Wakefield to do radio in the mental hospital meant Mum had to drive me there. If I wanted a tour of a radio station in Dublin while I was on holiday, Dad would go with me. We didn't have much money coming in so every extra thing was a big expense. My dad was a postman in Leeds for most of his life and didn't make that much money. Mum didn't have a job so his was our only income. My mum always hates me joking or telling stories about it but it's true. We weren't poor, but we were as near to poor as you could be without officially being poor.

I don't know what the Post Office paid my dad but the guy was always working overtime. If it wasn't for the fact that he used to pop in and see us if he was ever passing, I would never have seen him. (If Dad ever had a job that sent him near our house, he would drop in for a cup of tea. I wondered how he never got caught, bearing in mind there would be a massive juggernaut outside the house with 'Royal Mail' all over it.) He was always working overnights and long driving shifts. He said the work was easy because he enjoyed driving, but he did a hell of a lot of hours to make up for his rubbish wage.

Mum stayed at home and worked looking after the house and my brother and me, and that was really cool because we'd have a mum and tea to come home to. Lots of my mates at school used to go home and make their own tea. Stuff that! After a hard day's schooling, I expect my damn tea on the table by the time *Willo the Wisp* has finished.

I have a story about money, which my mum *hates* me telling. One day I was in the newsagent's with Mum and I saw a *Rainbow* comic. I loved the TV show *Rainbow* with Zippy, George and Bungle and I was desperate to get my hands on this comic. I begged my mum to buy it for me but she wouldn't give in. It was too much money and we couldn't afford the extra expense. The comic cost 50 pence. (Sorry, Mum, but this story really gets me sympathy!)

These days things are a bit better. I earn a decent wage and if my mum ever wants a *Rainbow* comic then I will buy it for her. She also has the best showbiz life a mum could wish for. Through my job in radio she has met half of the showbiz community. She is the *biggest* ligger I have ever met and she absolutely *loves* it. My mum has turned meeting famous people and having her photo taken with them into an art form. She has been to so many Radio 1 events that she's virtually assigned her backstage pass before I get mine. My mate Tim from Radio 1 nicknamed her VIP Vera.

FAMOUS PEOPLE MY MUM HAS MET IN THE LAST FEW YEARS

SIR CLIFF RICHARD Mum *loves* Cliff and has a nice photo of the two of them on the mantelpiece in the living room.

ANT 'n' DEC Again, several photos from several meetings.

NOEL GALLAGHER In Germany for the World Cup, I had to interview Noel. Just as we were starting the recording, my phone rang and it was Mum. She shouted hello and he shouted back, 'How are ya, luv?'

TRAVIS Mum is on first-name terms with all of them.

DAVE GROHL I have never met the lead singer of the Foo Fighters, but Mum has.

VICTORIA BECKHAM Mum gets a bloody mention in her autobiography.

VERNON KAY He loves my mum and dad.

DERMOT O'LEARY So does he!

TAKA HIROSE Mum is close friends with Feeder's Japanese bassist.

ROBBIE WILLIAMS During a rehearsal for a TV show I did, Mum walked in and Robbie shouted hello over to her. Then rehearsal stopped for them to have a chat.

CRAIG DAVID Mum will befriend anybody famous!

LOUIS WALSH He loves everybody Irish so he doesn't really count.

JERRY SPRINGER We all went for lunch one Saturday after the radio show. There's something not quite right about sitting with Mum and Jerry Springer in a London pub.

SHAUN RYDER Mum and my auntie Margaret spent hours chatting with him in a pub in Rhyl, north Wales. She had no idea who he was but said he was a charming man. He never swore once!

PINK Actually Dad introduced himself to her as 'Chris Moyles's dad'. She thinks he's gorgeous.

It's funny because my dad is a typical working-class northerner. He isn't fazed or impressed by much, but over the last year or so he's started to get into the whole backstage thing. Pink thought he was brilliant, which slightly annoyed me as I've been trying to cop off with her for years. If she ends up getting off with Dad I'll bloody kill him!

My brother Kieron is older than me and although we're similar looking, we are very different people. Kieron likes jumpers and trousers and I'm more of a shirt-and-jeans type of a guy. He has also always spoken very well, which is a polite way of saying he talks posh. Growing up we did the usual brotherly fighting thing but we always got on well. He liked different music to me and different TV shows, but over the years our tastes got more similar, which brought us closer together. He's also the most intelligent person I know. He knows *everything*. I swear that when we were born God gave me the talent of talking bullshit and being funny and gave Kieron every other skill and piece of knowledge ever. Up until recently he lived one street away from me and worked three streets away from Radio 1. He is really excited at the thought of me writing a book as he reads about ten books a week. I've read about ten books in my entire life! I just hope he bloody likes it.

2004 was my first year on the breakfast show on Radio 1. Sadly it was also the year in which my dad had a quadruple heart bypass and my mum got breast cancer. The greatest year of my career was the most worrying year in my personal and family life, but I suppose that's the way of the world. Dad is a strong character and got through his operation well. He's slowly getting back to his normal self, but we keep having to remind him that he's not a bloody superhero and he has to slow down occasionally – stubborn bugger!

Mum's breast cancer scared the shit out of me. I was with Sophie travelling on a train from Madrid to Seville when Mum called to tell me the news. It's a fucking horrible feeling. The chemotherapy was the worst bit for Mum. The breast cancer wasn't so bad, but the poison they stuck in her week in, week out almost killed her. She had all the usual side effects, including losing her hair, which hit her hard. I said I would shave mine off in support, but this only annoyed her. I suppose you wouldn't chop your legs off to support somebody who had lost theirs. I think she was a bit like: 'Look, I don't want to lose my hair. You choosing to shave yours off just makes me feel worse.' (Dad hasn't had much hair for years so he wasn't bothered either way.) All our friends were very supportive during this nasty time, but I did feel a bit sorry for my dad. Everybody would ask after Mum and send their best wishes, forgetting that Dad had just had a life-saving operation. Still, I suppose the word 'cancer' scares people more than the word 'quadruple'.

I live for my family and I'm not ashamed or embarrassed to say it. I love my parents and my brother so much that I honestly don't know what I'd do without them. I longed for this awful period to be over so that we could all sit down with a sigh of relief, knowing that the four of us were doing well. Christmas 2005 was the time. We all sat round the dining-room table having Christmas dinner. Dad was fine. Mum was fine. Kieron was fine, and I was fine. Ironically I'm the overweight, beer-drinking, cigarette-smoking lazy arse who doesn't do enough exercise, and I'm fit as a fiddle. It's the early mornings I think.

17

JUST
MY LUCK

N ow I know it's not just me, I know it's everybody. I can guarantee that your life is just as messed up as mine. Nothing goes smoothly, ever. Just when you think that you have something sorted, something else fucks up. It happens at work, it happens in your personal life, it happens all the time. You get home from work and all you fancy is a cup of tea or coffee. You open the fridge and you have no milk. You go out for dinner with some friends, having raved about how great the restaurant is, and on that night the service is rubbish, the food is cold and they try to overcharge you. You're in the car stuck in traffic so you decide to take a short cut and the journey ends up taking you even longer because of diversions and road works. Your favourite football team's on the television for the first time in ages, but some boring family or friends' event that you can't get out of clashes with the match. It happens all the time. It's never your fault, but you have to deal with it.

ALED IS AN IDIOT

Take my recent trip to Germany for the FIFA World Cup 2006. I've already mentioned that I feel as though I have a charmed life. I do a job I *love* where I laugh every single morning. I know there are people wandering around not knowing what they want to do with their lives and in the meantime stuck in a boring job they hate. This may even apply to you. It's one of the reasons I love doing the radio show every day. If I can make somebody who's driving to work to his or her shitty job laugh out loud just once, then I've achieved something that morning.

One of the perks of my job is broadcasting from somewhere other than the studio. Now I've said it a hell of a lot on air: these trips aren't a holiday. It's hard work. It's even harder than the daily studio shows because you feel you have to justify being somewhere different. So when we do the show live from New York, or Portugal for Euro 2004, or even Germany, the whole team works that little bit harder to make the shows even better. I have to say that I enjoyed being in Germany. The shows were even better than I thought they would be, with Dave and Aled recording some brilliant spoof travel guides and histories of the World Cup nations. Ben Cooper was on the phone every day saying how well he thought it sounded and what made him laugh that morning. Brilliant. We had achieved what we set out to do – what could possibly go wrong to take the shine off it?

ENTER MR ALED HAYDN JONES.

After the final Friday morning show we were due to drive about 300 miles north to a town called Herford. We had jam-packed all the people-carriers and vehicles with our bags and were fifteen minutes from setting off. Suddenly I hear some commotion coming from where the cars are parked. Aled, through no fault of his own, you understand, has fucked up. Big time. Aled has made a mistake that will keep us there for another ninety minutes and cost us 70 euros. Aled decided to put the air-conditioning on in his vehicle, so he opened the door, put the key in the ignition and started the engine, then he put the air-con on. Then he shut the door and somehow:

LOCKED THE FUCKING CAR WITH THE KEYS IN IT AND THE ENGINE RUNNING!

Unbelievable. We all had to sit around in the ridiculous hot weather for an hour and a half, waiting for a guy to turn up from the rental place to try and open the door for us. Eventually he did, by using a giant metal coat-hanger thing. The door was opened in twenty seconds.

THIS DAMN BOOK

Earlier in the week I had received a few messages from Claire, my book editor. Now at this point I had written about 50,000 words of the book, with only 20,000 more words to write. She had helped me a lot with the tone of it and the kind of things she thought I should write. When I called her she explained that she had something to tell me, which wasn't about the book, but would kind of affect it. She started the conversation and immediately I got pissed off.

'Now, Chris, you know right back at the beginning when you agreed to write this book, I promised you that I wouldn't leave the company?'

Now how the hell am I meant to respond to an opener like that?

'Yes I remember you saying that, Claire,' were my actual words.

'Well, the thing is, I'm afraid that I am going to leave, and I'm leaving in about two weeks' time.'

ARE YOU FUCKING SERIOUS?

Here was my book editor, my wife, mother, best friend and boss all rolled into one literary human being, dumping me for somebody else. How the hell was I meant to carry on now and who the hell was I going to trust?

'Well, there is a new girl who will be taking over and she seems really nice,' whimpered Claire.

'Oh well, as long as she's nice I suppose that's OK then, isn't it?'

So now as I sit here writing the book I have no idea what is going to happen.

SHOWBUSINESS EATING

There is a restaurant in London called the Ivy. It's been around for years and years and is a haunt for celebrities and the rich and famous. I've lived in London for ten years and up until recently had never been. All my friends have told me to go because I'd really like it. Even though a lot of famous people go there, it's very chilled out and the food is what I would consider normal. I don't eat much 'fancy food' and I'm always happy with a dish that comes with chips. Call me common, I don't care. I like what I like and apparently I'd like this place. My boss Ben Cooper decided to take me there as a bit of a 'well done' for having increased the listening figures again and for winning the Sony Gold Award for Entertainment. Now Dominic, who reads my news, has been there before and was sitting next to Sienna Miller on one side and the brilliant American actor Steve Buscemi on the other. Ben has also been before and seen movie stars and rock icons all tucking into their food, so I knew we were going to see some big stars when we went. Imagine the disappointment when I walk in and the first person I see is Vernon Kay having a business lunch. The only other famous person in there was the guy who used to present the *Police, Camera, Action* videos in the mid-1990s. On one side of me were an old couple who moaned every time I lit a cigarette and on the other were some suited posh business gentlemen who looked down their noses at me because I was wearing jeans. Stars my arse.

Incidentally I had the curry. It was very nice but had onions and I hate onions.

18

OUR TRIP TO GERMANY

You know I love my radio show and I love the team who work on it, but, trust me, after three weeks of working away in Germany with them, I'm ready to kill. I don't care which one of them I'd kill either. Aled is an option, as is Rachel. Jesus, I'd even kill Carrie and she's cute, but since spending time in Germany, I've seen more sides of these people than ever before.

ALED

I LOVE HIM, BUT HE'S STRANGE.

He gets all weird about spending too much time with the rest of the team and has to go off and have some 'on his own' time. However, unlike you or me, who would go and read a book or have a beer or sleep, Aled likes to go into the nearest big city and check out the local gay scene. Now he doesn't do anything that he's not supposed to, or so he says. He just likes to go and see what's going on. I have a theory that if Aled were straight, he would be considered a pervert. Because he's gay he gets away with murder. He goes to a gay bar, it's not a problem. The boys talk about going to a lap-dancing bar, we're perverts. Aled sees a twenty-two-year-old guy walk past and checks him out. If Rhys did the same to a twenty-two-year-old girl, he'd be an old pervert. He discusses Carrie's breasts in front of her and he's cheeky. I do it, and I'm rude and overly personal. You know sometimes I think he pretends to be gay just so he can stare at Carrie's breasts.

CARRIE

I LOVE HER, BUT SHE'S A WEIRD DRUNK.

On this trip we had a few nights of letting our hair down and having a few drinks. I stress this was a few drinks and not a marathon binge-drinking session. Normally it even revolved around food in a restaurant. Now we always take the mickey out her for being posh, but it's nothing compared to what she's like when she's had a drink. Her normal voice disappears and she begins to talk like she's a member of the royal family. Not only does she speak all posh but she also becomes fluent in gibberish. She starts to talk randomly about random stuff using random words and doesn't make any sense. On the night before her birthday she was laughing hysterically as she was talking, and nobody else at the table understood a word of what she was saying.

'Ha ha, oh my God, you know. It's just like Aled when he does the thing. He's a ha ha, you know. Oh it's so funny. Lamppost treacle trouser jumper!'

RACHEL

I LOVE HER, BUT SHE WINDS PEOPLE UP.

Rachel and Rhys fight like cat and dog. You'd think that they fancied each other the way they behave. But they don't, *trust me*. Every time they row it's the same. Rachel isn't very tactful and she also never knows when to leave something. Rhys is easily annoyed and wound up and tends to lose his rag with Rachel. Each one is the other one's nemesis. Rhys always thinks that Rachel is giving him a hard time; Rachel always thinks that Rhys is rude to her. It goes round and round and round and pisses me off. We're halfway through a 300-mile journey and have had to make a diversion because of traffic. We stop off at a petrol station in the middle of nowhere in Germany.

'I think we'll get moving and stop at the next motorway services,' says Rhys.

'How far away is that?' asks Rachel.

'I'm in the middle of Germany in a village – how should I know?' barks Rhys.

'I was only asking. There's no need to bite my head off, for God's sake.'

'I'm not biting your head off, I'm only saying I don't know because of this diversion. I'm not sure where we are so we'll just have to drive until we find one,' says Rhys.

'Fine, but there's no need to shout at me about it,' whines Rachel.

It never fucking ends!

RHYS

I LOVE HIM, BUT HE FARTS TOO MUCH.

He's the oldest member of our team and our executive producer. He is great at his job and has left his laddie days behind him. Well almost. His language and conversation round the dinner table can sometimes lead to the girls getting angry or upset with him. Sometimes they don't want to know about masturbation or chicks that shave themselves while they're tucking into their Caesar salads. But the worst thing is Rhys's flatulence problem. It's non-stop, twenty-four hours a day. The man is like a farting machine. He yawns, he farts. He stands up, he farts. He sleeps, he farts. He farted one morning while standing with his back to our breakfast table. If you ever moan about it, he just replies with the same line each time:

'It won't smell.'

I've never known anything like it in my life. There's so much gas inside that man that I'm amazed he smokes.

RICHARD EARL

I LOVE HIM BUT HE'S A SLEEPING PUSSY.

Richard Earl is a BBC engineer. He is probably one of the best outside broadcast engineers in the world. I'm lucky because I have worked with some brilliant ones in the past. Steve Richards is another but sadly wasn't on our trip to Germany. Instead it was Richard Earl and a guy called Nick Ford. They were both great, and technically brilliant. However, Richard likes a beer. I'm sorry, that's not fair. I like a beer, but this man is in a different league to me. Richard *loves a beer*. He also likes to sleep and the two seem to go very much hand in hand. I have never known a man who can fall asleep as quickly as this guy. Anywhere and in any situation, if Richard needs a sleep, it will happen.

At the dinner table.

At the bar.

In the car.

In the middle of a conversation.

He was talking to me while we were being driven back from town one evening. We'd had a few drinks but nothing excessive. Richard was asking me about Sophie's job. As I'm halfway through my answer, I can hear him snoring.

THE GUY FELL ASLEEP WHILE TALKING TO ME!

As I keep saying, I love my team and wouldn't have them any other way. But trust me, I'm ready to kill on a daily basis!

19

I HAVE BIRTHDAY PHOTOS

So by now you've gathered that I am bluffing my way through writing a book. I hope you like what you've read so far. I suppose if you hadn't liked it then you would have put it down or thrown it away and you wouldn't be reading this bit. I suppose, therefore, I can say what I like about those people, as they'll never read this bit, the boring, miserable bastards. Well, screw them. I have their money now and they ain't getting it back. So there.

Anyway, so just like normal books written by people who know what they're doing and keep the readers interested right until the last page, I have decided to put in some personal photographs. I called Mum and she sent me down a huge bag of them. Like most mothers, mine is obsessed with taking photos at any event whatsoever. It's my birthday, so Mum wants a picture. I make my first Holy Communion, so Mum wants a photo. I am wearing stupid shite ugly clothes because it's the early 1990s and I don't know anything about style yet, so Mum wants a photo. I trawled through hundreds of them and sent them to Claire, while she was actually still the editor of this book, and she chose her favourites. What will follow here is a series of photographs that range from cute baby pics to me looking like a beached whale asleep in a Winnebago. I'll put some captions up for the pics to give you a brief idea of what they are, but I think some of them need a bit more explaining, so here goes.

BIRTHDAYS

Mum has taken photographs at **EVERY SINGLE BIRTHDAY I HAVE EVER HAD**. Seriously, it's never-ending. This will be proved by the fact that there are no less than five different photos of five of my birthdays. This, however, I quite like because it:

A: *Makes you feel as though you were there, thus making us kind of friends, even though we'll probably never meet. And:*

B: *You get to laugh at how silly I look, how uncool I look and how my sense in style and clothes doesn't really kick in until well into my late twenties.*

MY DAD'S AWARDS FOR DRIVING

Now this may seem odd to you, but it doesn't to me. My dad drove vehicles for the Royal Mail for virtually all his working life, and he was bloody good at it. He taught my mum to drive and then taught me to drive and if it weren't for the fact that my brother is too lazy to learn, he'd have undoubtedly taught Kieron to drive too. (Incidentally, he doesn't work any more, so if anybody fancies learning, he does have some spare time on his hands and is very good too!) Because Dad was so good at driving, he was entered into the famous Lorry Driver of the Year competition. Drivers from all over the UK meet up and compete against each other to find *the* best lorry driver. Despite the fact that he never actually won the best driver in

Britain, he was very good and often came home brandishing other awards. I used to go and watch him reverse a lorry through some cones and various other hazards and applaud him loudly for finishing in a decent time. Anyway, there's a photo of him and me after one of these successful days.

VIRGINIA RHODES

She was the very first girl I ever fancied. One year at a birthday party at my house, Mum made us stand together for a photo. I don't need to write much more than that. I think you can work the rest out for yourself. The picture consists of a pretty little girl who looks a bit shy, next to a rigid, petrified young boy who is so embarrassed that his cheeks are glowing a bright shade of red. Unsurprising really, as I was twenty-five.

FUN RUNS

Despite the fact there is very little 'fun' in a 'fun run', I used to run quite a few when I was younger. They would be six-mile runs, or occasionally ten kilometres, which always sounded like a lot more to me. I'd run some of these with my dad, but I also ran a lot of them on my own. I wasn't the quickest runner in the world, but for some reason I always had a bit of energy left towards the end to make a final sprint over the finishing line. I would see it in the distance and increase my speed massively, firing through the other runners at a great pace, building and building and getting faster and faster until I was running so quickly I looked like a professional sprinter. I used to think this made me look good to the spectators at the finishing line. It didn't, of course, make me look like a serious runner because it had just taken me an hour to run a mile, and if I'd run the whole race at that speed I would've finished twenty-five minutes earlier. I don't have any pictures of me looking like a young Forrest Gump sprinting to the finish, but I have enclosed a picture of me looking soaking wet and knackered about four miles in.

I'M NOT FRIENDS WITH MARTINE McCUTCHEON

You will see a photo of me looking very fat in the face, standing with Mum and Martine. It was my surprise twenty-fifth birthday party in London. I showed up to a bar with a few friends and guess what happened? Yes, you guessed it, lots of people I wasn't particularly friends with shouted 'SURPRISE' when I walked in. Luckily there were also some actual friends I knew the names of. Later that night, and completely out of the blue, Martine McCutcheon walked in.

'Happy birthday, darling,' she said as she kissed me on the cheek.

'Oh bless you,' was my reply.

I had no idea what she was doing here. As it was a surprise party, I hadn't actually invited anybody to it, let alone Martine. Not that I was upset that she turned up. If anything it was the opposite. She was famous at that point and was also very cute, so all my pals thought that we were really close friends. I think it's fair to say that we had met maybe twice, and that the record company were passing the venue with her, mentioned that it might be nice to pop in and say hello, and so did. Mum didn't care less and reacted in her usual way.

'Oh, Martine, you look beautiful. It's lovely to meet you. Let's have a photo!'

IT'S NOT JUST MARTINE EITHER

It's anybody famous. My mum has been known to have her photograph taken with somebody famous, and then have the nerve to ask me who they were!

MOULDY LOOKIN' STAIN

For Comic Relief a few years ago, myself and the rest of the radio team ended up recording a parody version of Goldie Lookin' Chain's anthem 'Guns Don't Kill People, Rappers Do'. Penned by Dave and myself, it was entitled 'Dogs Don't Kill People, Rabbits Do', and we called ourselves Mouldy Lookin' Stain. We played the single a lot on the radio show and everybody liked it. The record company and the group agreed we could sell it for one week only with the proceeds going to charity. It was available as a download and we plugged the hell out of it on the air, despite the fact that *all* the money went to Comic Relief. Seven days later and we had unbelievably knocked U2 off the top spot, and as a result:

WE WERE ONLY BLOODY NUMBER ONE IN THE DOWNLOAD CHART!

We were so excited and pleased about the news that we completely lost ourselves. All rational thought went out the window and we all agreed to dress up as dogs and rabbits to perform the song live at a Radio 1 event in front of 20,000 people. We looked stupid but we delivered what the audience wanted: three minutes of comedy, and then we got off stage.

THE RADIO 1 ROAD SHOWS

These events were the tackiest, most crass and cheesy thing Radio 1 ever did, and they were brilliant. Thousands of people would gather on a beach to watch a DJ play records to them for an hour and a half. After my first year at the station, I was given my own week to tour five different seaside towns and do the show. As a joke I insisted on a Winnebago. The joke was on me before we even left for the first gig when I walked out of Radio 1 and saw a Winnebago sitting outside waiting to take us to Cleethorpes. The driver we had for the week was an old guy called Bob. He was soon nicknamed 'Scary Bob' on account of, in our opinion, the fact that he couldn't actually drive. Blind corners were not a problem for Bob, he would pull out to overtake a car and then come face to face with another car heading right towards us.

'Jesus, Bob, there's a car coming right at us,' we would scream.

'Yeah, I've seen it,' replied Bob, as we pull back into the correct lane taking the wing mirror of the other car. I found very quickly that the only way not to get scared during these journeys was to sleep. And so I did.

OH LOOK AT ME,, I KNOW BEYONCÉ AND ELTON JOHN

I interview a lot of famous people. Most of the time it's great, sometimes it's rubbish. It really depends on whether the guest is a knob or not. Luckily most people these days are fine. This is mainly due to the rule that we only have guests on the show we like. Please bear all this in mind as you look at me 'hanging' with the rich and famous. In most cases, they left the studio approximately five seconds after the photo was taken and I have never seen them again. However, it does look well wicked in the book and makes me look really popular.

MY GIRLFRIEND IS REAL, THANK YOU VERY MUCH

Finally there is a photo of Sophie and me together. That's because I love her, and she wanted to be in the book. (Like Vernon Kay, I am well aware who wears the trousers in the relationship, and it ain't the men!)

20

RADIO 1: ALMOST THE END OF THE BOOK

I woke up in the flat I shared in Baker Street. I was excited and not nervous at all. This was everything that I wanted to achieve; it was also the beginning of a new era for me. I had dreamt of this moment for years, since I was a young boy in my mother's kitchen at Christmas time. I had worked for my local radio station. Then I moved abroad to Luxembourg when I was eighteen. Then I moved home for a while as I worked in Bradford, then away again to Stoke-on-Trent and then further down the country to Milton Keynes. But now my travelling had finished. I had done what I dreamt of doing, something that hundreds of DJs like me also dreamt of. After seven years of working my arse off, today was the day. Today was my first day working for BBC Radio 1.

Some dream of being a rock star, or an astronaut. I was a geeky kid who dreamt of being a Radio 1 DJ. For me it was never a sad ambition, it was a cool one. Stepping through the doors of Radio 1 for the first time as a DJ for me was the equivalent of a footballer walking through the doors of their favourite club or walking out onto the pitch at Wembley for the first time.

Today, Monday 21 July 1997, was going to be my first day in the office. I left Baker Street and hailed a taxi. Bizarrely, the first cab to stop was a bright yellow one advertising Capital Radio. I walked through the doors at Radio 1. I was immediately unimpressed. The reception area was like that of any boring office anywhere. It wasn't flashy or impressive like Capital Radio's building. There were no pictures on the walls of the DJs past or present, and it was so small there was hardly anywhere to sit. But I didn't care.

In that first week I met a lot of people, including Simon Mayo, who had always been a hero of mine.

'When do you start, Chris?' he asked me one day outside the building.

'Monday morning,' I replied with a smile on my face. I smiled because he knew when I was starting – he'd refused to play the trail advertising my show because it had an ad-lib line from me at the end saying:

'Can I say the word "penis" on Radio 1?'

Over the next few days I met Nicky Campbell, with whom I would later have a *massive* argument. I met Jo Whiley, who nodded her head at me as I walked past. And I met the legend that was John Peel, who was a miserable old git! He made a comment about me being like DLT-in-waiting and I made a nasty quip back. I was told, point blank, that John was out of bounds when it came to comments like that. A few years later at a Radio 1 DJ dinner thing, someone came up to me at the bar and pinched my arse. I turned round to see John looking at me.

'Was that you?' I asked, thinking that it couldn't have been.

'Yes it was,' he said, smiling back.

'Oh right, erm, in that case, can I buy you a drink?'

'Yes, please,' he said.

That night John and I talked properly for the first time. We spoke about many things. Music, football and, more tellingly, his family. He told me how proud of them he was and how much he loved them all. He had a tear in his eye as he spoke and admitted that it made him cry thinking about them because he loved them so much. I spoke about my family and by the end of it I think I had convinced him that I wasn't the arsehole he probably thought I was. I was devastated when he died. He was a great broadcaster and I wished I had known him better.

My first show on Radio 1 was Monday 28 July 1997, on the 'early breakfast' show. Four o'clock in the morning until seven o'clock. I loved it. I didn't love getting up at three in the morning, but I really enjoyed the show. I was twenty-four then and the show was very 'tits and arse', as Zoë Ball said one day, but I loved it. We had people come into the studio and we'd try to get them naked. We had a woman fake an orgasm on the air, which I then mixed over some classical music. A band called Rialto or something released a record called 'Monday Morning 5.15' so we got them in the studio to play it live one Monday morning at exactly 5.15. It was never a hit!

After the first producer left, Ben Cooper took over. Ben was brilliant and we did a lot of funny things on the radio. Jude Adam was the assistant and was, to put it mildly, very confident. She was the last person you wanted to see at four o'clock in the morning. She went to bed early to get her eight hours of sleep, so when you saw her first thing she was alert as anything. Ben occasionally picked her up and drove her into work. He would also sometimes pick me up on the way in. I remember standing on the corner of Baker Street at 3.15 in the morning watching Ben's car approach. I was shattered, grumpy and cold. As Ben's car got nearer, I noticed Jude sitting in the front passenger seat waving jauntily like a child.

'And a very good morning to you, Mr Moyles. How are you on this lovely morning?' she beamed as she wound the window down.

'Fuck off,' I replied.

At this point I understood why I'd been told to fuck off for being chirpy early in the morning. I swear if it weren't for the fact that we were so tired doing that show, Ben or I would have killed her! She was brilliant at her job, though, and got the best phone callers ever. It's a skill trying to find somebody awake enough at 4.30 in the morning to play a surreal radio game. Thanks, Jude.

With the addition of Comedy Dave to the team, the early show lasted for fifteen months. It was hard work getting up five days a week in the middle of the night. It did mean that I had most of the day free, but I hadn't been in London for that long, and most of the people I knew worked during the day. So what does any self-respecting twenty-four-year-old do all day every day?

SPEND ALL DAY IN THE PUB OF COURSE.

And we did. Every day Dave and I went to the Horse and Groom on Great Portland Street and pretty much stayed there all day. I don't know how I never became an alcoholic. The pub opened at 11.30 in the morning and most days we would be the first in. We had our lunch in there and I even slept on the couch in the back room some days. Remember, I didn't have anywhere else to be, and nobody to be doing anything else with. In the early mornings we'd speak to thousands of people on the radio and then have nobody to play with during the day. After a while it became apparent to anybody who worked at Radio 1 that Dave and I would always be in the pub, so it quickly became a meeting place for lots of the staff. Some would pop in on their way to work, some for lunch, and a good few people would call in after work for a few beers with us. We must have single-handedly kept that bloody place going. And it was a Sam Adams pub so it was all their own brand and that lager was strong!

The early bit, as we called it, was going well despite the constant lager. Features included 'True or False' and the brilliantly titled 'What's the Word or Words'. Then we replaced the missing-words feature with a competition where the caller had to answer the previous question. It was a quiz-game version of a classic Morecambe and Wise *Mastermind* skit, and I loved it. Dave and I couldn't come up with a name for it so we opted for something that had no relevance to the actual feature, and 'Viaduct' was born.

Halfway through my time on the early show, I was given a sixth show at the weekend: Saturday mornings at 6 a.m. Oh, thanks for that. I'm on at 4 a.m. Monday to Friday and now 6 a.m. on a Saturday. Luckily we were moved to 10 a.m. on Saturdays shortly after, and some people said that they were the best shows we did. Dave and I would roll into the studio, normally still a bit drunk from the Friday night before, and talk rubbish and giggle for a few hours. Everybody loved it. Dave and I were so tired from the week that we never really wrote anything for it. It was all ad-lib. We always said that if we had actually put any effort into the show, then it could've been huge!

One day Andy Parfitt called me to say he was changing the schedule around and we were to be put on the afternoon show. This was great news. Finally we could stop boozing during the day and have some sort of a normal life. Our last early-morning show was Friday 2 October 1998. Thank Christ!

Ben Cooper produced the show, with Dave assisting in place of Jude, and me at the helm. I felt that I was going to set the world of radio on fire, and so I made a big opening sequence featuring my American voiceover friend Paul Turner's booming voice over the top of the classical music piece *Carmina Burana*. It was typical Chris Moyles subtlety.

Last year he proved to the UK that he was the saviour of early-morning radio.

Now the battle is about to begin.

Welcome to your worst nightmare.

The saviour of afternoon radio, Chris Moyles.

Nicely understated, I thought! I knew that other DJs would be listening to see what we were like and so I had a message for our competition too:

Bob Geldof, Doctor Fox, whoever the hell's on Virgin today. Disc jockeys around the UK beware. We have arrived.

Start as you mean to go on, in my opinion! I had dumped my car-salesman agent and moved to ex-Radio 1 DJ Bruno Brookes. Bruno was a funny bloke but he tried his best. He got us more money and started building a good relationship between me and Andy Parfitt. Originally the show's start time was 4 p.m. We were only on until 5.45 p.m. It wasn't even a two-hour show, which actually made it very difficult to do. Eventually we got moved to 3 p.m. and everything was going great.

The show tried out different musical intros, and we ended up with a Green Jelly rock track, which I'd always liked and planned on using for years. Paul Turner's booming voice would announce the day and the time, 'and now live from London, it's Chris Moyles'. After a while Ben left to go and produce Jo Whiley. He wanted to stay with us but thought that he better not say no to management when they asked him. I went through various producers until in November 2000 we found Will Kinder, a.k.a. Grey Ed, on account of the fact that he had grey hair. (I am a comedy genius.) Will was the butt of many jokes and features, including my personal favourite, called 'Bang Will's Head Against the Studio Window'. It even had its own sing-a-long jingle. We took Will, put a crash helmet on his head, and then proceeded to bang his head against the studio window. After that came 'Fire at Will', where we threw stuff at his head (he continued to wear protective headgear). Will called a halt to this feature after Dave threw a battery at him and Will said it hurt. Great times! Will once spoke about me very fondly in an interview with *Heat* magazine.

'If you were ever in a fix and Chris could help, he would. That's not to say there aren't times in the studio where I'd happily put his face through the window.'

It was during the afternoon show that I started working with Jon Culshaw, whom I'd met briefly at Capital. Jon is the *best* impressionist in the business. He had started out doing voices for *Spitting Image* and by now was making a big name for himself. Jon and I bumped into each other in my local pub and started chatting about work and stuff. We hit it off immediately. He was currently helping Steve Penk do phone wind-ups for Capital but told me that he wasn't the happiest there. I asked him if he was tied to a contract (like I was some kind of big businessman luring people into my special company!) and whether he'd fancy doing any voices for our show. By coincidence I was filling in for Kevin Greening and Zoë Ball on the breakfast show the next day and we had the first play of the official England song for Euro 2000. So we basically stole Jon to come in and do some of his brilliant football impressions, such as Alan Hansen and Gary Lineker. Soon after that Jon was with us every week doing impressions and annoying real celebrities by pretending to be them. (Chris Eubank called in one day to complain that it wasn't the real him on the air. Jon spoke back to him as Eubank!) Jon and I still see each other regularly and we often accompany each other to TV shows or events. I went to watch Jon get interviewed by Michael Parkinson and he was brilliant.

We spent five years doing the afternoon show and it was, on the air anyway, a great time. Off the air, however, we had problems. A certain member of Radio 1 staff wasn't as keen on the show as I'd have liked. They made a point of telling me that they didn't understand Dave's role on the show and that maybe I should try doing the show without him. This particular person also said to my agent that I would 'never, ever, present the breakfast show on Radio 1'. (Sorry about that, luv!) But it's true that there was a time at Radio 1 where it was just horrible to work there. A few people at the BBC saw Dave and me as a couple of dangerous idiots who shouldn't be allowed on air. Luckily Dave and I rode through it all and things started to get better. We even started to win some awards for the show, despite every radio critic hating my guts.

On 30 September 2003 I was due to go for a social drink with Andy Parfitt, the controller of Radio 1. I had been at the station for six years and my relationship with Andy had gone from being almost non-existent to really good. We had a trust thing going where we could talk to each other about the show and be really honest with each other. He called me before the afternoon show to explain that he had to go and look after his children for a few hours while his wife worked, but that he could meet me about eight-ish. Ben Cooper was now back at Radio 1 after having been away for a while, and he was Andy's number two man. This was so pleasant after the few years of trouble that Dave and I had had before. Ben and I always got on well so he suggested a few beers first before I met up with Andy. Looking back I can see it was the biggest set-up ever. Ben and I met up and chatted a while, then he got a call on his mobile and told me Andy was round the corner in a hotel bar. Ben and I left the pub and then he announced he had some work to do, but would join us later. Fair enough, I thought. As he left me he smiled at me and said, 'Have fun.'

Have fun? What's he on about? I'm going for a drink with my boss, not a lap-dancing convention. I took a deep breath before walking into the hotel to see Andy. After the usual chitchat we sat in a quiet corner. Andy had a sly grin on his face, and I hoped he would say what I wanted to hear.

'Chris,' he said in his ever-soft tone. 'You and I have really come a long way in these last few years. We've got a mutual respect and I think there's a lot of trust there too.'

SAY IT.

'Remember when I asked you to calm down before, because if I ever had plans for you I didn't want them disrupted?'

SAY IT.

'Well, I'm very happy with the way things have worked out for both you and me, and while I was away the other week I did a lot of thinking about the station and about you in particular.'

JESUS, SAY IT, FOR CHRIST'S SAKE.

'So I've decided that I'm going to put you on the breakfast show.'

JESUS CHRIST HE SAID IT.

This was *everything* I had ever wanted since I was eleven years old. I took a breath, smiled and simply said, 'Thank you, Andy.'

In the cab on the way home my phone beeped with a message from

Andy. It said, 'Chris, thanks. That was an historic meeting. Call me tomorrow when you get up. Best Andy.'

It was 10.24 p.m. I know because I still have the text on my phone. I am a bit of a geek.

Ben and I talked about who we wanted for the show and that was that. The next day I had to keep my gob shut for the whole show as *nobody* was allowed to know. Eventually when I told Rachel, she was delighted. This was her text:

'Wow, I'm going to be producing the Radio 1 breakfast show! How exciting! I'm shattered. Congratulations, it's about time! See you tomorrow. Rach X.'

I kept that one too. Well, I thought it was sweet.

My first Radio 1 breakfast show was on Monday 5 January 2004. I had spent a while with my friends Sandy Beech (yes, it is his real name, stop asking) and Roger Dexter at their Music 4 studios helping to produce the new jingles for the show. We decided for a laugh to make the longest ever jingle to start the show. It was more like a song really, telling the history of the breakfast show, with clips of some of the ex-DJs. Some of the lyrics included:

'Since the days of Simon Mayo things have never been the same again.
And the breakfast show since ninety-nine has had a notable lack of men.'

Referring to Sara Cox and Zoë Ball, who had previously presented the shows. It was just over five minutes long and was brilliant in its understatedness! I started the show with the jingle and then played the

Move and 'Flowers In The Rain', which was the first song ever played on Radio 1. (Jesus, I am *so* sad.)

Over the next few weeks we pulled out all the stops. The shows even by my standards were funny and entertaining. The critics made their usual comments but I was feeling very confident. When our first official listener figures came in, we had added over 600,000 new listeners to the show. By the end of the year it had reached about one million.

The second year at Breakfast and things were even better. I started to receive awards at proper ceremonies that people had actually heard of, including the GQ Men of the Year awards. Now, almost three years in, the show has gained a reputation for being one of the best breakfast shows ever on Radio 1.

That accolade came from me, by the way, and has yet to be endorsed by anybody else!

So here I am living my own dream. I've been working for Radio 1 since 1997 and I still get a buzz when I walk through the front doors. I remember as clear as yesterday my first show and I still enjoy working here. In fact, that's an understatement. I *love* working here. I don't care if it sounds a bit wet – I do *love* my job. Every day I get to hang out in a studio with people I really like and have fun. I'm paid to laugh every single morning. How many people can say they laugh at their job every single day? I'm fairly shy in real life, so it's nice when people tell me how much they love the show. Even chants of 'Moylesy, ya fat bastard!' are nice to hear. Not always, you understand. I mean, if you see me at a funeral, please don't be tempted to shout.

So there you have it. The story of how I dreamt of being a DJ in my mum and dad's house and then became the host of the breakfast show on BBC Radio 1. I hope you've enjoyed my book and thank you for reading it. (I'm not sure if I'm meant to thank the readers, but, as I said at the beginning, I've never written a book before so take it as the nice gesture that it is!)

God bless you and have a safe journey home.

Chris Moyles, 2006

BACK

WORD

The first time I heard about Moylesy was when I was going to do an interview with him for the afternoon show, and a couple of people warned me he could be a bit tricky. What did they mean, 'tricky'? I think what they meant was: butt-clenchingly honest, willing to take the piss out of himself and to take the piss out of you, and unable to fawn over someone if they start annoying him. Think Halle Berry. Yes, I suppose that does make Moylesy a bit tricky, but it's why I listen. He's a genius. Just check out his show and you'll see for yourself. I had the great pleasure of giving him his *GQ* award, and a few months later he gave me a *Glamour* award (how lovely) and he said, 'She's done some really great shows and she's also done some real rubbish.' You see? Incapable of bollocks. (Although ,obviously that *is* bollocks.) And he has an amazing knowledge of music. Any track enquiries, and he is always the first person I call. Usually at some incredibly inappropriate time.

My most special moment, which I shall owe Moylesy big time for the rest of my life, was when Carlos Bernard (Almeida in *24*) was on the show. I am a huge *24* fan and, if I'm honest, a huge Almeida fan … he's hot.

So I hear he's on and start frantically sending Moylesy texts from the school car park about how much I love him and how my ringtone is the phone ring from *24* ... all sad fan stuff ... and then start driving home. After the next song Chris says, 'Have you heard of *Big Brother*?' I get very excited. Carlos says yes. Chris says, 'Well, the host of *Big Brother* has been bombarding me with texts about you.' And he proceeded to read them out, which was very embarrassing. And then he said, 'Shall we call her?' I try not to crash as I go into spasms trying to find somewhere to pull over. I am actually sitting there listening to them call me and I am staring at my phone, waiting. Then the *24* ringtone starts. I pick up the phone and it's Almeida on the other end! OH MY GOD ... HOW AMAZING IS THAT?

If you are not a *24* fan, it's not amazing at all, but it made my year. I went a bit funny. Moylesy even said, 'You sound all weird,' but I was just speechless.

Chris has become a good friend and I think the sun shines out of his jacksy.

Davina McCall, 2006

THE

LIST

Many friends have casually asked me: 'Am I mentioned in the book?'

They say they are only joking and that they're not bothered, but of course they are. Who wouldn't want their name mentioned in a book? As well as this, there are many people I just haven't had the space to write about. So with that in mind, I have compiled a list of names for you, the reader, to peruse at your own convenience. The list is a mixture of:

Actual friends of Sophie's and mine.

People I have worked with or admired.

Celebrities I have met and liked.

Celebrities I have never even met but like anyway.

And, to fill the list out a bit, random names of people who may give me discount if I put their name in my book.

So that's the set-up, and here are the names.

MADONNA	*She's cool.*
TONY BLACKBURN	*He did it before anybody else.*
WILLIE THORNE	*Legend with a tash.*
JIM AND LISA	*Sophie's brother and his wife.*
JOHN PEEL	*RIP.*
GREG YOUNG	*Crazy lad with no hair.*
HOOP DOG	*Takes pictures for the website and is funny.*
WILL KINDER	*Grey Ed.*
PATSY KENSIT	*Blimey. She's fit and likes the show!*
TIM 'RUP DOG'	*a.k.a. Tim from accounts.*
JK AND JOEL	*Bless them.*
TONY BYRNE	*Eh, it's me, Tony Byrne.*
ERIC MORECAMBE	*Partner to Ernie Wise.*
RICHARD MURDOCH	*Ex-producer of mine and a nice man.*
HOWARD STERN	*Genius.*
DR MARK HAMILTON	*The most rock 'n' roll doctor ever.*
PAUL ROBINSON	*Not the one from* Neighbours *but the goalie.*
WOODY	*Signed for Real Madrid and got us tickets.*
DAVID HEALY	*Hobbit.*
CHRIS WORTHINGTON	*Bald.*

JAMES CHAPPELL GILL *Boing boing boing.*

LIZZIE *Worked with me at Radio 1.*

MITCH JOHNSON *Friend of mine with a beautiful voice and a big willy!*

ANDREW CAREY *The landlord.*

PAUL MARWOOD *Friend since nursery.*

PAUL DURANT *Friend who asked, 'Am I mentioned in your book?'*

MARTIN KILLKENNY *At school I thought he looked like 'Midnight Caller'.*

JOHN KELLY *School friend who now lives in Japan – cool.*

BILLY BREMNER *Leeds United football legend.*

PAUL TUNNELL *Sophie's friend who looks like Ali Campbell from UB40.*

EMMA PONTEY *Friend of mine I once almost saw naked!*

ANDI PETERS *TV star and man with ego bigger than mine!*

ROLAND RAT *And Kevin the gerbil as well.*

SIMON HIRST *Ask him how to pronounce the word 'horse'.*

SISSY AND NELSON *Sophie's niece and nephew!*

SOPHIE'S MUM JILL *Self-explanatory.*

UNCLE JIM *My dad's brother and Yorkshire legend.*

AUNTIE MARGARET   *Married to my dad's brother.*

SUZIE KANE   *Cousin in Ireland who is nice.*

ALL MY IRISH FAMILY   *Hello to all of you as well!*

KEVIN McNULTY   *Friday night Kevin from my local pub – love him.*

CLIVE WARREN   *Used to present children's TV with a stuffed dog.*

TATTOO DAVE   *Friend who looks like he could kill you, but he's lovely!*

JODIE AND ABBIE   *Our cute friends who are childhood sweethearts. Bless.*

JON CULSHAW   *Best impressionist in the world and good friend.*

ELECTRICIAN ALEX   *Odd man, but did a brilliant job.*

ACCOUNTANT DEREK   *He really is called Derek.*

ROGER @ MOJO   *The best bar in Leeds and Barbados.*

RICHARD PERRY   *Supports Spurs. Can get you anything, but not dodgy.*

AL JAMES   *Ham!*

VICKIE AND JAMIE   *Alfie Robbins's mum and dad.*

DORIS AND TREV   *Sophie's nan and granddad.*

UNCLE TREVOR   *Sophie's uncle that I call uncle too. Painted our wall.*

TIM AND MIM	*Nice neighbours who are sweet.*
MICK COHEN	*Legend from Leeds who sings the best karaoke ever.*
MARTIN O'BYRNE	*On on on.*
KIM AND FOZZIE	*Our friends. One's a Jew, the other's black. Wicked!*
KATRINA FOX	*Fancied her at school.*
LEG H	*First time!*
RUSS ABBOT	*Met him in Portugal. Comedy legend.*
ZOE AND NORMAN	*She's cool. He's cool. Bastards!*
RICHARD AND JUDY	*Book club?*
MAX BEESLEY	*All my female mates fancy him. I just like him!*
RACHEL UNITT	*Gorgeous girl plays football for England. So cool.*
TALL PAUL	*Tall DJ and nice holiday companion.*
DAVID O'LEARY	*The original Good Morning Jingle recipient.*
RICHARD BACON	*He's dippy and very intelligent too. How?*
PATRICK KIELTY	*Funny. Generous. Likes a drink. I like him.*
NOEL GALLAGHER	*Hero of mine and friend of mine. How cool is that!*
TRAVIS	*Love them.*

EMBRACE	*Love them.*
NIK KERSHAW	*Love him more 'cos he was my first live concert.*
PAUL McKENNA	*Helps me not freak out on planes. I'm not mad, though.*
MATT LUCAS	*Always sweet and very nice in real life.*
DAVID WALLIAMS	*Matt's working partner!*
BO SELECTA LEIGH	*Married to my ex. Nice guy, but nuts!*
THE OSBOURNES	*Apart from Jack as he lost weight and I'm still fat.*
JOHN FRIEDA	*£70 for a haircut? Piss off.*
HUGO SPEERS	*Brilliant actor, top fella.*
FEARNE COTTON	*Beautiful, talented, sexy, not interested in me!*
BIG GEORGE	*Composer and genius man. Honestly.*
PAUL TURNER	*My American voiceover man. Amazing.*
PETER TAIT	*RIP.*
KENNY EVERETT	*Wish I could have met him. My radio hero.*
SANDY BEECH	*Shit name. Brilliant producer. Great friend.*
SPENCE MACDONALD	*Friend from Stoke days. We drank and laughed lots.*
SCOTT SHANNON	*Legendary DJ in New York.*

DARYL DENHAM *Hardest-working DJ I ever met. Funny too.*

TREVOR *Floppy Jelly (don't ask).*

SIMON ROSS *The party animal. Roar.*

MARTIN KELNER *Excellent broadcaster. Stolen his lines before.*

MARK AND LARD *Brilliant. Thanks for putting up with me.*

WESTWOOD *Respect Mr Big Dog.*

MICHAEL GRECO *Chelsea fan but apart from that, he's cool.*

NEIL HANNON *I loved the Divine Comedy.*

ADRIAN TREDINNICK *Thanks again for the help.*

ICE CUBE *Not his real name.*

ROGER HARGREAVES *He invented the Mr Men. How cool is that?*

MR BUMP *My favourite one.*

GEORGINA BOWMAN *Read my news for five years in the afternoon.*

CHUCKLE BROTHERS *You can't have one without the other.*

RICHARD OLIVER *Man who sings the jingles on the Chris Moyles Show.*

EVERYBODY ELSE *Hello to you all.*